T0142554

GOD
is in the Business of Picking up the
PIECES

Edward Mutema

WESTBOW
P R E S S®
A DIVISION OF THOMAS NELSON
& ZONDERVAN

Scripture quotations are from The Holy Bible, English Standard Version®
(ESV®), copyright © 2001 by Crossway, a publishing ministry of
Good News Publishers. Used by permission. All rights reserved.

Good News Translation® (Today's English Version, Second Edition)
Copyright © 1992 American Bible Society. All rights reserved.

Scripture taken from the King James Version of the Bible.

Scripture taken from the *Amplified Bible*, copyright © 1954, 1958, 1962,
1964, 1965, 1987 by The Lockman Foundation. Used by permission.

Scripture taken from the Holy Bible, NEW INTERNATIONAL VERSION®.
Copyright © 1973, 1978, 1984, 2011 by Biblica, Inc. All rights reserved worldwide.
Used by permission. NEW INTERNATIONAL VERSION® and NIV® are
registered trademarks of Biblica, Inc. Use of either trademark for the offering
of goods or services requires the prior written consent of Biblica US, Inc.

WestBow Press books may be ordered through booksellers or by contacting:

WestBow Press
A Division of Thomas Nelson & Zondervan
1663 Liberty Drive
Bloomington, IN 47403
www.westbowpress.com
1 (866) 928-1240

Because of the dynamic nature of the Internet, any web addresses or
links contained in this book may have changed since publication and
may no longer be valid. The views expressed in this work are solely those
of the author and do not necessarily reflect the views of the publisher,
and the publisher hereby disclaims any responsibility for them.

Any people depicted in stock imagery provided by Thinkstock are
models, and such images are being used for illustrative purposes only.
Certain stock imagery © Thinkstock.

ISBN: 978-1-5127-3076-0 (sc)
ISBN: 978-1-5127-3077-7 (hc)
ISBN: 978-1-5127-3075-3 (e)

Library of Congress Control Number: 2016902388

Print information available on the last page.

WestBow Press rev. date: 02/24/2016

Contents

This book is dedicated to my late father and mother-in-law, Benjamin and Chengeto Gudza, who became my mum and dad in every way. Their love and devotion to God I will treasure for the rest of my life. They looked after the broken all their lives, and their legacy lives on.

Acknowledgements

I would like to thank my lovely wife, Tererai, and my wonderful children, Bongai, Gareth, and Janice, for being there for me.

To Bishop Joshua Dhube and his wife, Lillian, for their spiritual parenting from the beginning.

To None Mugano for continuing to inspire me through her commitment and dedication to God's work through community project initiatives that have helped many.

To Cecil and Naomi Myambo for their support and prayers for my family over the years.

To my churches, UBC/UK and Holy Trinity, for their encouragement and fellowship.

Author's Testimony

I have been there. Broken. In pieces. This is the reason why Jesus matters to me more than things. I have seen friends on the edge. Crumbling. At the tipping point because of the loss of a loved one, a broken marriage, an errant son. Devastated and unable to pick themselves up.

None of us can boast about anything, because we all fall short. We have never met God's standard, but the good news is that he has met his standard on our behalf. It doesn't make sense. It defies logic, yet this is the greatest narrative that has ever been told. God in man reconciling the world to himself. He has put a high value on each one of us. No wonder why he cannot let us go.

Writing this book has helped me reflect on the important things of life. A life freely given, a character freely reconstructed, and broken pieces tenderly put together. The sum total of everything is who I am, and hopefully who you are or can become when you finish reading this book. Enjoy!

CHAPTER 1

God Is in the Business of Picking up the Pieces

We have all been broken at some point, sometimes damaged beyond recognition, helpless and hopeless and unsure if we will rise again. But God uses others to save broken lives. His salvage team is ready to respond at short notice, just as he has done all through the ages. He is there for you today, tomorrow, and always.

When the children of Israel were in dire straits, he sent Moses. When the Jews faced possible extinction, Esther gathered courage to face the king. And Jesus, in the story of the Good Samaritan, shows how one from the enemy camp rescued the man who had been left for dead, and a new definition of neighbour was born.

Whatever situation you are facing, God has you covered. If you are by the brook hungry like Elijah, the widow of Zarephath will pop out to give you her last meal. Maybe in the pit like Joseph, the Ishmaelite will buy you and take you to Pharaoh. Or if you are a Daniel in the den of lions, God will shut the lions' mouths and deliver you. God is always on the lookout. He is vigilant, like when Daniel was thrown into the lake of fire. There appeared one like an angel, the fourth man to quench the fiery furnace. What a mighty God he is. And he says through David, "Because he loves me, I will protect him." His angels are on duty twenty-four/seven to ensure that nothing happens to us. This God is worth considering. He is worth serving and worth worshipping. He is dependable, trustworthy, and faithful.

Read on, and get ready to face head-on the challenges that have broken you in the past. Stand tall and claim your position. Consider yourself undefeated. It's a new day!

All of us will be broken at some time in our lives. That is the reality of life. We should anticipate this and be ready when it comes round. Be prepared before the day comes. Paul says, "Therefore take up the whole armour of God, that you may be able to withstand in the evil day, and having done all, to stand firm" (Ephesians 6:13 ESV). Get ready before the battle. Resolve yourself. Equip yourself. Get as much information as you can get to prepare yourself to take on the vagaries of life: the tsunamis, the twisters, and the other violent storms that must come. Don't wish them away, for they will surely come. That is how it has been from the beginning. The calm was there before the creation of the world. Afterwards, it was chaos, trials, and tribulations. This is a fact. It is unavoidable. Instead of being caught by surprise, be ready for battle. What is your role? You must be prepared for the winters and the violent storms when they come.

And these storms spare no one. Jesus was led into the wilderness to be tempted by the Devil, even though he was full of the Holy Spirit. Your position in Christ is no guarantee that you will be spared. But you can be ready. You can arm yourself with God's weaponry. You can withstand. Like Paul, you can say,

> We are afflicted in every way, but not crushed; perplexed, but not driven to despair; persecuted, but not forsaken; struck down, but not destroyed; always carrying in the body the death of Jesus, so that the life of Jesus may also be manifested in our bodies.
>
> (2 Corinthians 4:8–10 ESV)

The reason is that we are carrying this treasure in us that enables us to withstand the schemes of the Evil One. We should be able to emerge from the rubble of our brokenness. Strive for the propensity to survive from mangled wreckage following a horrific accident on the highway. It is possible. This is inexplicable but possible. We can get married after a messy relationship that tested our belief in the concept of love. We can see our son or daughter, whom many had written off, become a man or woman of great integrity. It is possible. With God, nothing is impossible. And as God said to Jeremiah, "I am the LORD, the God of all mankind. Is anything too hard for me?" (Jeremiah 32:27 NIV).

Brokenness spares no one. It includes the rich, the poor, the powerful, the vulnerable, leaders, and followers. In the sea of brokenness, people lie in anguish and sorrow hoping to get back to wholeness. It is not for a lifetime. It can only be for a season. Sometimes we wait in expectation, ready to go through the season. And it is difficult to anticipate the gravity of it all, but you must stand ready to deploy the spiritual arsenal already prepared. This includes the Word of God, prayer, and your faith and trust in God. Paul says,

> For the weapons of our warfare are not of the flesh but have divine power to destroy strongholds. We destroy arguments and every lofty opinion raised against the knowledge of God, and take every thought captive to obey Christ.
>
> (2 Corinthians 10:4–5 ESV)

Brokenness is not despair. It can lead to it, but not necessarily. You cannot teach it, you can learn from it. Your experience can lift others higher. It can bring hope to the hopeless and life to the lifeless. It fools the Enemy. When a spear was thrust into Jesus's side at the cross, blood and water oozed from the side. The Enemy thought that was the end. And three days later, Jesus emerged from the tomb stronger and more powerful. He was ready to lead the world to victory. You may have your Achilles' heel from where the Enemy launches his attack, but when you are weak, that is when you are strong. Out of the depths of despair, the power of God is demonstrated. The woman caught in adultery felt done by, but Jesus lifted her up. Zacchaeus may have sunk in the quicksand of corruption, but at Jesus's invitation, he experienced God's love. The Prodigal Son had reached the end of his tether, but he came to his senses and was welcomed home like a prince.

Even death ceases to frighten us. As Paul says, "For me to live is Christ and to die is gain" (Philippians 1:21 ESV). The fear of death is real when we are broken, yet what matters most is to hold on to the foundations of our faith. Paul faces death squarely when he says, "O death, where is your victory? O death, where is your sting?" (1 Corinthians 15:55 ESV). There is no need to despair when we are broken, no need to lose heart when we are crushed by the rigours of life. The only way is hope, faith, and tenacity. There is no fear in love. But perfect love drives out fear because fear has to do with punishment. "The one who fears is not made perfect in love" (1 John 4:8 NIV). And Paul says,

> "Since therefore the children share in flesh and blood, he himself likewise partook of the same things, that through death he might destroy the one who has the power of death, that is, the devil and deliver all those who through fear of death were subject to lifelong slavery."
>
> (Hebrews 2:14–15 ESV)

Death has always been the Devil's trump card. In many cultures, it is so feared that people will do anything to hide or minimise its occurrence. And when one suffers from a terminal illness and there seems to be no way out of it, the fear of death cuts out even the faintest hope one had, and one sometimes dies *before* one dies. No one has the right to pronounce despair on another unless the person allows it. You are your own liberator, and you should dictate the terms and conditions for your today and your future. Brokenness is not despair but can be a conduit for the rise and rise of the broken, the disheartened, and the hopeless. Are you?

Brokenness is not a curse. It is a season, an experience. This is the stuff that we go through as men and women who have made a commitment to follow Jesus. It is to be expected. We should anticipate it. We should not be taken by surprise. We should prepare for it. It should not embarrass us and is not a signal that all is not well with our lives. When it comes, we should take the bull by the horns and go through it. You will not be the only one with this kind of experience. Many have gone through this before, and many will do so long after you are gone. Heaven is the only place where brokenness is non-existent, because the mender of broken souls lives there, and by the time we get there, the job will have been done. This was done when Jesus cried, "It is finished." We were made whole then, and all we need is to claim back our wholeness whenever it is threatened.

Jesus was cursed on our behalf. He took our curse. Now we are free. We experience freedom even when we are broken. Like David, we can say, "My flesh and my heart may fail, but God is the strength of my heart and my portion forever" (Psalm 73:26 ESV). Job says, "As for me, I know that my Redeemer lives, and at the last He will take His stand on the earth.

Even after my skin is destroyed, yet from my flesh I shall see God" (Job 19:25–26 ESV). We can affirm our trust in God even when we are broken. Our confidence may be rekindled, our faith soaring, and our hope unfading. Don't be fooled. Brokenness is not a curse.

Brokenness is legitimate. Share it and propel others to greater heights. David did it, and his testimony brought many from the brink. Paul hammered the point at every opportunity, and his testimony changed the world. Yours can too. Here are some of David's testimonies:

Surely God is good to Israel, to those who are pure in heart.
But as for me, my feet had almost slipped;
I had nearly lost my foothold.
For I envied the arrogant
when I saw the prosperity of the wicked.
They have no struggles;
their bodies are healthy and strong.
they are free from common human burdens;
they are not plagued by human ills.
Therefore pride is their necklace;
they clothe themselves with violence.
From their callous hearts comes iniquity;
their evil imaginations have no limits.
They scoff, and speak with malice;
with arrogance they threaten oppression.
Their mouths lay claim to heaven,
and their tongues take possession of the earth.

Therefore their people turn to them
and drink up waters in abundance.
They say, "How would God know?
Does the Most High know anything?"
This is what the wicked are like—
always free of care, they go on amassing wealth.
Surely in vain I have kept my heart pure
and have washed my hands in innocence.
All day long I have been afflicted,
and every morning brings new punishments.
If I had spoken out like that,
I would have betrayed your children.
When I tried to understand all this,
it troubled me deeply
till I entered the sanctuary of God;
then I understood their final destiny.
Surely you place them on slippery ground;
you cast them down to ruin.
How suddenly are they destroyed,
completely swept away by terrors!
They are like a dream when one awakes;
when you arise, Lord,
you will despise them as fantasies.
When my heart was grieved
and my spirit embittered,
I was senseless and ignorant;
I was a brute beast before you.
Yet I am always with you;

you hold me by my right hand.
You guide me with your counsel,
and afterward you will take me into glory.
Whom have I in heaven but you?
And earth has nothing I desire besides you.
My flesh and my heart may fail,
but God is the strength of my heart
and my portion forever.

> Those who are far from you will perish;
> you destroy all who are unfaithful to you.
> But as for me, it is good to be near God.
> I have made the Sovereign LORD my refuge;
> I will tell of all your deeds.
> (Psalm 73 ESV)

David spells out the reason why he was broken, the issues he had to grapple with, and how he resolved this dilemma with the help of God. And finally he tells the world what he would do with such an experience. He says, "I will tell of all your deeds." David turned his brokenness into an inspiring story of his life, which he used to help others appreciate the goodness of God. Will you do the same, when the season of your brokenness is over? Don't be selfish. Go and tell it. Pass on the good news!

Paul had a similar approach. He says,

> "Indeed, we felt we had received the sentence of death.
> But this happened that we might not rely on ourselves

but on God, who raises the dead. He has delivered us from such a deadly peril, and he will deliver us again. On him we have set our hope that he will continue to deliver us, as you help us by your prayers. Then many will give thanks on our behalf for the gracious favour granted us in answer to the prayers of many."

(2 Corinthians 1: 9-11)

David echoes similar sentiments in Psalm 34:18 (NIV). "The LORD is close to the broken-hearted and saves those who are crushed in spirit."

It is when we are broken-hearted, wounded, and in despair that the light of God shines through. It is when we are at our most vulnerable that sometimes we defy all odds against us and plod on. Our test becomes our testimony, and our weakness becomes our strength. We find our way through the quagmire of our failures. This is maturity. It reflects a grasp of what brokenness can mean if we embrace it rather than resist it. But it is tough.

When you are broken, remember to fight depression. You are at your most vulnerable when you seem to have lost all hope and nothing seems to be going right for you. The world seems to have crushed into your head. You cannot think properly. Nothing seems to make sense. You feel down, lonely, and on the verge of utter helplessness. This is the moment when alarm bells should ring. You say to yourself, "I need help. I am going to win this battle." And seek help from God and those who have the skills to get you through the experience, through counselling, prayer, encouragement, or all of these. Job is a classic example of someone who was exposed to God, his friends, and his dear wife. All giving their input to try to help Job deal with his situation. After everyone had given their piece of advice, Job made an informed choice and got over his despair and despondency. He makes a great statement of faith.

"For I know that my Redeemer lives, and at the last he will stand upon the earth. And after my skin has been thus destroyed, yet in my flesh I shall see God" (Job 19:25–26 ESV).

Instead of being depressed, Job comes to the conclusion that God remains God, alive and well, and that his purposes will stand. Nothing will affect his authority and power. His ability to resolve the mysteries of life remains intact. What an attitude. What faith! What hope!

God picks up the pieces. That is what God does best. He creates, recreates, and transforms. He makes things new. He redoes things. He remakes, reshapes. That is his nature. "And he who was seated on the throne said, 'Behold, I am making all things new.'" Also he said, "Write this down, for these words are trustworthy and true" (Revelation 21:5 ESV).

He remade me. He transformed me. This book is awash with examples of such reconstructs. People who messed up but whom God patched up and made whole. He can do this in an instant. He does this through a process along life's journey. He is in the salvage business. Wow!

I am one such piece. He brought me from the gutter into his marvellous light. And he will do it again and again.

When people cry to him, he hears their cry. He responds to the broken.

It is a paradox. He is a loving God, but he is also a jealous God. He is a righteous God, yet he hates evil. But when he looks at you, he always shows mercy. That is why he mends the broken-hearted, day in day out.

It may have happened in your childhood. You may have just lost a loved one without saying goodbye. You may be on the verge of a breakdown. Lost for words and not knowing when it will happen. There is someone who understands. He is a friend who can bear our sorrows and grief. He is the one who guarantees to deal with your issues not just today or tomorrow but for eternity. He has a track record. Many millions have found solace in him. Many in the Bible proved him right. And today, he remains relevant in the slums or the corridors of power.

This song sums it up:

> God is still on the throne and He will remember His own
> Though trials may press us and burdens distress us, he never will
> Leave us alone for God is still on the throne.
> And he will remember his own
> His promise is true, He will not forget you
> God is still on the throne
>
> (Lyrics by Mrs FW Suffield)

This is the story of our lives. Every day. This is why we were not created as zombies but as flesh and blood. We think, we react, and we have faith in today and tomorrow.

God uses our enemies to launch us to greater heights. For a season. He did it with the children of Israel. It was part of his strategy. No wonder why Jesus says the following about enemies:

> "You have heard that it was said, 'You shall love your neighbour and hate your enemy.' But I say to you, Love your enemies and pray for those who persecute you, so that you may be sons of your Father who is in heaven. For he makes his sun rise on the evil and on the good, and sends rain on the just and on the unjust."
>
> (Matthew 5:43–45 ESV)

And Paul says to the Romans,

> "Live in harmony with one another. Do not be haughty, but associate with the lowly. Never be wise in your own sight. Repay no one evil for evil, but give thought to do what is honourable in the sight of all. If possible, so far as it depends on you, live peaceably with all."
>
> (Romans 12:17 ESV)

You are not your own, for you were delivered at a price, as a follower of Jesus. It means you are unique. You are under his protection and God will use every means to make you recover from your current predicament. To make you rise up and walk. Enemies are in this equation. That is what God does. No limits. No holds barred.

The story of the Good Samaritan is a classic example of how God uses our so-called enemies. The Samaritan had compassion on the man. Not only did he make sure that his wounds were cleaned and oiled; he also ensured that he was taken care of until he fully recovered. Those the man expected would come to his rescue, passed by. God is innovative. He is creative. He is concerned with the end result. Your salvation. Your restoration. Your wholeness. And anyone can be an instrument for your survival. Including enemies. Wow!

He did this too in the Old Testament.

> I am sending Assyria against a godless nation, against a people with whom I am angry. Assyria will plunder them, trampling them like dirt beneath its feet.
>
> (Isaiah 10:6 NLT)

It's true that God sent a heathen nation, the enemy of the people of God, to fulfil his purposes. When you are broken, when you are done and think no help is coming, take a cue from what God did to his people. Your enemy can be used to bring you to that place where you appreciate who God is. This is a place where you can experience God's deliverance. The earth is the Lord's and the people thereof. So he does what he wants with those he has created in order to accomplish that which he has purposed. God has a helicopter view of our lives.

He sees from the beginning to the end. So his resolution of our challenges takes the end in consideration. We are blinded because we only see the here and now and not tomorrow, not through eternity. He hardly discloses what is to happen except in rare occasions when he reveals it to his chosen prophets.

Why will God use your enemy to accomplish his purpose? This was a question the prophet Habakkuk struggled with. He could not understand such an irony in the running of God's kingdom. How dare he, God, do this when he knows how our enemies have devastated our nation?

"Look at the nations and watch—
and be utterly amazed.
For I am going to do something in your days
that you would not believe,
even if you were told.
I am rising up the Babylonians,
that ruthless and impetuous people,
who sweep across the whole earth
to seize dwellings not their own.
They are a feared and dreaded people;
they are a law to themselves
and promote their own honour.
Their horses are swifter than leopards,
fiercer than wolves at dusk.
Their cavalry gallops headlong;
their horsemen come from afar.
They fly like an eagle swooping to devour;

they all come intent on violence.

Their hordes advance like a desert wind

and gather prisoners like sand.

They mock kings

and scoff at rulers.

They laugh at all fortified cities;

by building earthen ramps they capture them.

"Then they sweep past like the wind and go on—

guilty people, whose own strength is their god."

Habakkuk's Second Complaint

LORD, are you not from everlasting?

My God, my Holy One, you will never die.

You, LORD, have appointed them to execute judgment;

you, my Rock, have ordained them to punish.

Your eyes are too pure to look on evil;

you cannot tolerate wrongdoing.

Why then do you tolerate the treacherous?

Why are you silent while the wicked

swallow up those more righteous than them?"

(Habakkuk 1:5-13 NIV)

It is God's prerogative to do what he desires. And when you go through the valley of the shadow of death, you know that God can raise salvation from any quarter. He is not limited by time or space. Remember he created the universe out of nothing. His word was enough to make what was not into what was. And John the Baptist reminded the Pharisees of this fact.

And do not presume to say to yourselves, "We have Abraham as our father," for I tell you, God is able from these stones to rise up children for Abraham.

(Matthew 3:9 ESV)

And it is equally true that God can raise your deliverance from anywhere and anybody, including your enemies. You need to be open about it. Expect it from all corners. And embrace it when it comes. Do not despair. Keep believing. Keep hoping. Keep the faith all the time.

Not only does God use our enemies to deliver us; he uses our friends as well. One friend can make a difference between life and death. David testified to this. Jonathan, his bosom friend, rescued him from Saul, his father, several times. This was one of the most intriguing relationships in the Bible. And when David then became king, Jonathan's son was rescued from obscurity to the limelight of dining with the king for the rest of his life.

As soon as he had finished speaking to Saul, the soul of Jonathan was knit to the soul of David, and Jonathan loved him as his own soul. And Saul took him that day and would not let him return to his father's house. Then Jonathan made a covenant with David, because he loved him as his own soul. And Jonathan stripped himself of the robe that was on him and gave it to David, and his armour, and even his sword and his bow and his belt. And David went out and was successful wherever Saul sent him, so that Saul set him over the men of war. And this was good in the sight of all the people and also in the sight of Saul's servants.

(1 Samuel 18:1–5)

Real, genuine friendship is scarce currency today. Many befriend others for selfish reasons. For what one can get and not for what one can give. David and Jonathan's friendship was unique. Jonathan loved David as his own soul. Wow! Jonathan could die for David. And God can use your genuine friends during his salvage business when he decides to restore you to your original self. Thank God for friends. And you too must be a friend God can use from time to time, to make a difference to other people's lives.

You see, our God is a strategist. He has the master plan. He has crafted myriad options for the people he has created in order to achieve his objectives. He never is pleased that any of us perish perilously. His rescue options are at the ready and will be applied appropriately to make the maximum impact.

While we plan and seek to wriggle out of our brokenness, in the end, it is what he has planned that will succeed. We are responsible for partnering with him in resolving our situation, but he has the final word. Yea or nay belongs to him. That is favour. That is grace. And we will always be grateful for what he has done. Take heart; be of good courage, for Jesus, who is the champion, has overcome the world. He triumphed against all odds. And as he told the disciples, "He who endures until the end will be saved." It is all about enduring in tough times.

This is the stuff that heroes are made of. And God honours those whose focus is on him, the "Author and Finisher of our faith." Can you say hallelujah?

You may feel abandoned, left out. Remember God has not abdicated his throne.

CHAPTER 2

God Is in the Salvage Business

David rose to stardom from shepherding sheep. He won battles. Dined with kings and lived on the edge. He messed up. Took someone else's wife and killed her husband. David became a liar and a murderer. A prophet uncovered his sin. What a shame. He ruined his reputation and let God down, big time. Today, he would have been written off and his political life in ruin and never to take public office again. Remember Richard Nixon?

And suddenly, David confesses. He acknowledges his sin before God. He asks for forgiveness. He seeks restoration. And God accepts him. He shows mercy on him. He welcomes him again into his camp. But he still suffers the consequences. The child born out of adultery dies. And David again is ranked by God among the great heroes. He is given the title "a man after God's own heart" (1 Samuel 13:14 ESV). Wow! It's like David's life is put on the replay button. A broken life put together again.

Hannah was the love of Elkanah's life. But she had no children. His second wife was blessed with children. She was Hannah's problem. She taunted her for not having children and this left Hannah distraught, distressed, and sad. But she was a woman of prayer. She believed in a God who answered prayer. She was consistent. She was dedicated. Her priest got confused when he saw her lip-praying. No sound but praying from the heart. He thought she was drunk. She was pouring her heart to God. She was a prayer strategist. Her prayer was simple. "Give me a son and I will dedicate him to you for the rest of his life" (1 Samuel 1:11 ESV). God answered her prayer. Samuel was given to God and stayed in the temple. He became one of the greatest prophets of all time. Hannah acknowledged this in her song. God promotes the poor to dine with the rich. Another broken piece back in its place.

On Easter Friday, Jesus hung on the cross. Bleeding, weary, and abandoned. But he had company. Two thieves hung with him—one aggressive and another empathetic. They deserved their punishment. A just conviction. They knew that was the end. But one remembered who Jesus was. He made his appeal, "Jesus remember me when you are in your Kingdom" (Luke 23:42 ESV). The response was immediate. Access was guaranteed in Paradise immediately! This was a complete turnaround. That is how God restores people. However broken they are. It can be micro-oven instant! Today, Jesus responded. Not tomorrow. Not after a ceremony. Not before a priest. Are you broken? Take a cue from the thief. And Jesus is not a stone's throw away. He is here and now. Burdens are lifted at Calvary. Who has broken you? Is it a husband, a wife, an errant child, or bereavement? Is it baggage you have been carrying forever? Now is the time to resolve, to dump it on someone who has gone through it all. There is no formula. You say it, acknowledge it, and seek help to deal with it. It's not easy. It is hard work, but it is worth it. The thief on the cross seized an opportunity. Next stop, heaven!

He was treated like a celebrity. He was a murderer. But he was arrayed before the crowds because Pilate the governor had to present two prisoners before the crowds. They had to choose one per tradition. Only this time one was a murderer and the other had done nothing wrong. The verdict seemed clear-cut. Barabbas was destined for the gallows. Not quite. Pilate thought so. Not the crowd. "Free Barabbas!" they shouted. Not Jesus. Not the one squeaky clean, but the murderer. It looked like justice in reverse.

Barabbas set off for home, hesitant and unbelieving. He knew he did not deserve such a sentence. He was grateful that someone stood in the gap. What sort of person would do this? Why did he do it? Many people have asked these questions over the years. But this is the nature of God. He will show mercy to whoever he wants to show mercy. It is his prerogative. He is indeed in the business of picking up the pieces. While Barabbas dined that night with his family, Jesus was hanging on the cross. Aren't you grateful? I am.

She was a lady of the night for many years. The community knew her. She even went for married men. She had had many husbands previously. Her conscience was seared. She couldn't care. She was a woman of the city, until she met her match: Jesus of Nazareth.

He offered to fetch water for her from the well, which was a strange gesture by a man at that time. She was introduced to a man who could guarantee her water for life. She was a Samaritan, and he was a Jew. A contradiction, as these two were not the best of neighbours. There was animosity between them.

He asked her to call her husband. And she was dead honest. She had five! Her life was in tatters. She had been exposed. But he offered her life—quality life. And she went wild with joy. She ran straight into the city. Told everyone what Jesus had told her. And she spread the good news of life even to the men she had affairs with. Broken but reconstituted. She lived a full life again. How broken are you? Trust God, and he will do the rest.

Many men and women today are in a fix. They are caught up in unhealthy relationships. They are desperate to come clean. They are broken and battered. There is still hope. He is a master craftsman. He specialises in mending you.

He waited for thirty-eight years. We are not told how old he was. He waited patiently. He was not able-bodied. No wheelchair. No assistance. At the pool, there was a hive of activity. Everyone sat expecting something to happen. Unannounced, an angel would stir the pool. Those who dipped in the pool at that moment were healed instantly. It looked simple. Dash for the pool and you are OK. Then the big question: "Do you want to be healed?" asked Jesus. What? The man has been stuck at the pool for thirty-eight years?

This gentleman's explanation was that many jumped over him. He stood no chance, unless he flew over them! Jesus came and confronted him. "What do you want me to do for you?"

"To be healed."

"Well fair enough," Jesus said to the man. "Stand up and walk."

And he walked. He was transformed. He did not need an angel. He got healing from the King of Kings, the one who created angels. Wow! When the time had fully come, he was healed. When your time comes, God will put the pieces together and make you whole. It's been too long, but the time is now.

A pastor friend on the verge of great leadership responsibilities messed up. He had a relationship with a girl and that was sad news for the church. My response was "God is in the business of picking up the pieces." He sinned. Period. For many, he was now a write-off. But not with God. He remains God's child. That is God's verdict.

Joseph had everything going for him. This was at age seventeen. He was loved. He was a dreamer. And his future was almost guaranteed. His concern for his brothers changed all this. They were the enemy from within. They planned to get rid of him. They were jealous. And while Joseph was in the pit waiting to die, they had a meal, until the Ishmaelite showed up. Joseph ended up in Egypt, becoming a servant of Pharaoh. When Pharaoh's wife accused him of rape, he ended up in prison. The end, one would say. But suddenly his interpretation of prisoners' dreams took him back to the palace. This time he arrived as a prince and not a prisoner. A disintegrated life was made whole again. As this was not enough. God used his influence to save the nation of Israel. Wow! That is God for you. He doesn't see pieces but wholeness. He does not see a wreck but a recovered soul.

She was beautiful. Her beauty hardly noticed. She was a slave girl in a foreign land. Her people were doomed, on the verge of being exterminated, until the king initiated his own beauty contest. He decided to put the queen on display. All girls took time off to prepare themselves. On the appointed contest day, the queen refused to show up. She defied the king. Esther won the contest and became queen. She gained instant promotion.

The leadership was not happy. They decided to plot against the queen's people. An edict was passed. A day was set to execute the decree. It backfired. The mastermind of the scheme ended up on the gallows. Esther's intervention before the king saved a nation. And her uncle echoed those famous words, "Who knows why you were born at such a time as this?" (Esther 4:14 ESV). God's mercy was shown at the right time. What seemed impossible became possible. Have faith in God. You will survive. You will not be broken.

We all have an Esther moment. God places us strategically in order for us to make a difference, transform a person, a people, and a community. While daggers are drawn against us, we survive. We stand the test. And you realise your purpose. Why are you here "for such a time as this"? Writing this book at this time is significant. A story, a book, an audience, and a heart changed for good. We are all books to be written. We are all stories to be published. For we have a story to tell. Esther wanted to be silent. She did not want to be involved. She wanted to take the back seat, until her cousin gave her a stark reminder. If you don't step up to the plate, that is not the end of the story. If you refuse to intervene, God will raise someone else. He is not bereft of people for the moment. He raises game changers willing to do for God what he has purposed all their lives.

A great challenge, wherever you are. You can save a generation by serving a generation. Esther saved the Jewish nation. See what impact the Jewish people have made to the world of religion, art, science, and business. This can be traced back to that Esther moment. You are made to make a difference. And God can pick you up and help you realise your dream.

She was a professional hustler, a prostitute. Well known in the neighbourhood, until the people of Israel showed up. They sent spies before attacking the city. She hid them when the city men went after them to kill them. She refused to disclose their whereabouts. They promised her freedom, together with her family. The city was destroyed, but they were saved. Her name remains in the history books. She was broken morally, but God used her for the deliverance of a nation. Can he use you, in your current state? Yes.

Dr Paul in the Bible was an "educated fool" before he met Jesus. He persecuted Christians. He was ignorant of who Christ was, until he confronted Jesus. This was on the Damascus Road. In Syria! He stood no chance. "What do you want me to do?" he asked Jesus. The assignment was clear. Take the message of Christ to those that were hitherto excluded, to royalty and to the most influential people around. What a great challenge. But first it was preparation time for the task ahead. The strategy was to be filled with the Holy Spirit. To be baptised. To go and fulfil the task God had set for him. From a sinner to a saint. From a fool to a force to be reckoned with. All this was done through the power of Jesus. What seemed to be a wasted life turned to be God's investment. Paul's education, passion, and zeal were now to be used for the propagation of the gospel. His writing skills came in handy as Paul's letters became some of the most influential for generations. And lives were transformed as a result.

And Paul would always declare, "I am what I am by the grace of God" (1 Corinthians 15:10 ESV). This was what translated Paul's foolishness into the wisdom of God. From ashes to dining with kings. From brokenness to wholeness. And the formula is still the same for everybody. Today, tomorrow, and forever. When we have given up on ourselves, and others think the same, God says, "Hang on. I created you, and I can recreate you." And he does. David prayed, "Create in me a new heart Oh God, and put a right spirit within me" (Psalm 51:10). He did, and he still does. God's love endures forever. He does not write people off. He has no favourites. He is patient. He is in the business of transforming people. And when he does, it's huge.

Paul exuded so much confidence that he was able to declare, "We are more than conquerors." He was prepared to take on Satan, the challenges of his time, for the sake of the gospel. And he was prepared to die for the cause of Christ. " For me to live is Christ, to die is gain" became his swansong. Paul had confidence, tenacity, and passion emanating from a man who hitherto had been spiritually broken and was "the chief of sinners." It is possible when our hope is built on nothing else but Jesus Christ and his righteousness.

Peter was an efficient fisherman until Jesus called him to fish for people into the kingdom. He was outspoken, impulsive, and weak on reflection. He sometimes jumped the gun. He lied when convenient but remained passionate. Jesus understood Peter and gave him the benefit of the doubt. When he denied Jesus, I am sure he thought that was the end for him. But Jesus had faith in him. He prayed for him. He knew Peter was under attack. And Peter came back, full of the Holy Spirit, to lay the foundations for the early church. He now had substance, boldness, and passion.

Think of pastors who have failed God and their families but decided to start again. Business people, politicians, doctors, and athletes have done the same, but God is in the business of picking up the pieces. He raised them up.

The man at the pool of Siloam had almost given up, until Jesus turned up. The question was direct. What do you want me to do? What is your predicament? And with a typical stress response, the man gave Jesus a lecture. Don't you know? Can't you see? But eventually he gave the right response. He wanted to be healed. He had tried, but unsuccessfully. You may consider hard done by. No exit to your situation. Jesus is very precise. He wants to know what it is that you want done. Not what has happened before. He is not interested in what may have been and what could have been. He wants to know now what you want: getting a new job, to restore my marriage, to heal me, to have an intimate relationship with him, etc. Lay it on the table, and he will walk with you to accomplish the mission. It is hard work. It may not be instant. You have a responsibility. The lame man had to take up his mat, stand up, and walk away.

We are all at the pool, waiting. She was an alcoholic waiting to dry out. She had tried and tried. She'd been to the best dry-out centre in the land. She sat under the feet of great carers. She has always promised that this time she will stop forever, but forever never comes. It comes back again and again. Tomorrow seems not to come, and even when it does, it's like yesterday. She sings her 1970 favourite, sitting on the porch of the dry-out house: Yesterday must be forgot No looking back no matter what There's nothing there but mem'ries that bring sorrow Yesterday is gone, gone but tomorrow is forever. ("Tomorrow Is Forever" by Dolly Parton). Tears run down her dry cheeks. Her eyes turn reddish. She can't focus. Her head goes into a spin. She can't remember yesterday. But today is the problem. She is down. She has lost hope. It's like sitting at the pool, waiting for a deliverer. But he seems delayed. Or is he not turning up? Perhaps he has forgotten her. Her mate is clean now. He has a job. He is going to church. He may become a preacher. He has left the pool. Wow!

You see, the pool is her place of hope. She sits there in expectation. She does not know how long. Some have been there for years, day in day out. Every day is different. One day, she hears rumours of the coming One, the Deliverer, the Saviour. Everyone stands ready. Some look up. Some look down. There is an air of expectation. But this has been going on for ages. Hope is fading, and doubt is filtering in.

These episodes of hope and despair, so near yet so far, kept coming to Risa. Convinced that she was going to be OK, she kept banging on a door that muffled the sound so no one could hear. She kept screaming without an echo. No one seemed to hear. Her voice turned husky until she was inaudible. Only her thoughts kept saying, "I want to dry out. I don't want this anymore." But there was no audience. She was all alone with her thoughts, her feelings, and her frustrations. But she was still at the pool, with loads of people around her yelling and screaming. It was a deafening sound.

You see, we are all at the pool. This is where life is sorted. Problems resolved and burdens lifted. But you have to take one step into the pool. At the right time, when the signal is given, you should muster the resolve to do it. You have to have the resolve to do it, on your own. You have to push through the crowds. You should dash for it, when the roll is called out. When your name is called, you must respond.

God goes for the one and not the hundreds: lost sheep, lost coin, lost son. He goes for the crumbs and not the bread. God targets the despised and not the honoured and the broken, not the mended but the sick, and not the healed. Jesus was taunted for doing just that. "The Pharisees and the teachers of the Law started grumbling, 'This man welcomes outcasts and even eats with them'" (Luke 15:1 GNB). Jesus was different. His teaching is still different today. Today a stigma is attached to anyone who has committed a crime. They can't shake it off.

It is a point of no return. Will they be forgiven? Nada! Once perceived a murderer, always a murderer. The world seems to have no capacity to forgive as Jesus did, to embrace but not condone, to forgive, to restore, to heal, and to forget, as David says about God. "As far as the east is from the west, so far does he remove our sins from us" (Psalm 103:12 GNB). Not only that, but he remembers them no more. Ouch! Hebrews 8:12 (NIV) says, "For I will forgive their wickedness and will remember their sins no more."

I guess that is why he is God and not man. His love is so big you can't get over it. This is his core business. The first couple, Adam and Eve, messed up humanity, but he restored it on Easter Friday. During the time of Noah, people behaved like animals having sex with celestial beings. Then swoosh! The floods came and erased mankind as we know him, but the rainbow signalled a new existence, the new nation under Noah and his lot. God came to the rescue once again. He showed patience, tolerance, and abounding love. Until today, the rainbow is a reminder of how God continues to fend for mankind.

Below is a poem I wrote in 1989.

The Rainbow in the Sky

Always glaring in the sky,
A constant reminder that we are one,
Forever one.
African, Chinese, Caucasian, Asian—you name it.
Tell it to our children, we will.

When they ask what makes us one,
We will always point to the rainbow in the sky.
There, written in heavenly ink,
Painted in heavenly crowns,
The message is loud and clear:
One nation, one people.
A unity in diversity.

God's rainbow still shines, even when we have gone through tragedy and difficult times. You hear stories of people who lost entire families in a car accident yet they still thank God for what happened. A couple I knew many years ago lost three members of their family yet was still able to rejoice and to help others who were facing similar tragedies. There is in us the capacity that can only be God given to stay focused and not allow yesterday to ruin our tomorrow. Compare God's response to our response.

> Brothers and sisters, we do not want you to be uninformed about those who sleep in death, so that you do not grieve like the rest of mankind, who have no hope. For we believe that Jesus died and rose again, and so we believe that God will bring with Jesus those who have fallen asleep in him.
>
> (1 Thessalonians 4:13–14 NIV)

The focus here is on tomorrow. The expectation is that though tragedy may come and we lose loved ones, there is hope.

Hope in the midst of despair is the story of so many who were addicted to drugs and alcohol. Years later after they seek help, they come to their senses and become active, hopeful, and precious members of the community. Wow!

You see, there are no write-offs in God's world. Are we going to be judged? Yes, you will suffer the consequences of your action, but beyond that, there is room for improvement. You can come back home. You are guaranteed acceptance. In fact, in the parable of the lost or Prodigal Son, it was "celebration time" when he finally came to his senses and came home. Is this not kind of weird? Aren't you grateful you are not God! Uh!

Lazarus was Jesus's best friend. And so were his two sisters, Martha and Mary. Then disaster struck. Or was it? Lazarus became ill, and when the report came to Jesus, for some reason, he delayed. He did not respond quicker and stayed where he was for a further two days. For Martha and Mary, this was the end of their brother. Their only hope, Jesus, wouldn't budge. Impatient, confused, and fed up can only describe their feelings.

Lazarus was pronounced dead. And then Jesus appears. He reassures the two sisters. He tells them that their brother's death was for a purpose. This was to show the glory of God. What?

Don't give up. God shows up in ways that we cannot understand. As we throw in the towel, God steps in. His solution appears. He picks up that which is on the verge of collapse. He rescues that which the world has deemed to be at a point of no return. The "I give up" moment becomes the recovery moment. The "That's it" moment becomes the opportunity for

God to demonstrate his power. He is the lastminute.com God. Just at the nick of time, he pitches up and does extraordinary stuff. The religious leaders were mesmerised. They became jealous. This was not in their book. This was going against their tradition. And when the supernatural takes over the natural, the natural man cannot understand it. This is the moment when the mind cannot comprehend what is going on.

You are significant, even when you are broken.

Insignificance becomes significant. That is the story of the history of the Bible. From Genesis to Revelation. And the appearance of Jesus from Nazareth who became the ruler and Saviour of the world baffled the world: from a manger to a mansion in heaven. When Nathaniel heard about John preaching about Jesus, he made the famous remark "Can anything good come from Nazareth?"

Joseph came out from herding sheep to the king's palace. David was a shepherd boy who ended up being the best king Israel ever had: "a man after God's own heart." Daniel was a mere teenager when he was taken to Babylon with his friends and ended up as the most important ruler—wise and honest. Nehemiah was only a servant in the king's palace but ended up rebuilding the walls of Jerusalem. Joshua was Moses's assistant who took Moses's mantle and led the people of Israel into the Promised Land. Can anything good come out of Nazareth?

Some situations seem bleak and beyond repair. Certain prejudices come to the fore. Just like Nazareth was despised. Yet out of this seemingly impossible situation came the Saviour of the world. What the world saw was not the insignificant

Nazareth but the significant Jesus who came to seek and to save the lost.

It may seem like stretching it when you ask, "Can anything good come out of my dire situation? Can my brokenness, my illness, my broken relationship mean anything?" The answer is yes. You have history on your side. Many struggled with pain and diseases, but God was faithful and they came through. Scarred, bruised, but stronger, more resolute, and blazing with testimonies of God's goodness. And the result was that many others in similar situations were encouraged and their spirits lifted up as a result.

Jesus goes on to tell Nathanael, "You will see greater things than these. You will see heaven open, and the angels of God ascending and descending on the Son of Man." And whether Jesus is talking to Nathanael about the day when he would ascend to heaven after his resurrection or the time when he will come again with the angels from heaven at the end of time, his words also capture something beautiful about the way that our eyes can be opened by God when we are converted from our cynicism into faith in the reality of his kingdom. We too can see heaven open when we look at the world through the eyes of faith. The word for "angel" in Greek—αγγγελος—can refer to the supernatural creatures that surround the throne of God, but it can also mean just "messenger." God is sending us messengers all the time! God is always using people in our lives to encourage us, to challenge us, and to test our faith, all for the purpose of drawing us into a closer walk of discipleship with him.

When we examine closely our situation, we will see God at work in us. We will notice that all things work together for good to those that love him. A closer look will reveal how even in the midst of turmoil, God's purposes are being fulfilled. Yes, something good can come out of an awful situation. You may not see it until Jesus comes by and reveals it to you. Nathaniel said, "Come and see," referring to Jesus, who was close by. There is something about Jesus who, in the midst of Nazareth, will transform the situation. Nazareth appears ordinary and unimpressive, until Jesus shows up. Your situation becomes desperate until you cry to the Author of life who created you in the first place.

You cannot define God. We can never understand his ways. The so-called wise man of this world cannot comprehend such wisdom. As Paul says,

> For the message of the cross is foolishness to those who are perishing, but to us who are being saved it is the power of God. For it is written:
> "I will destroy the wisdom of the wise;
> the intelligence of the intelligent I will frustrate."
> (1 Corinthians1:18-19 NIV)

Brothers and sisters, think of what you were when you were called. Not many of you were wise by human standards; not many were influential; not many were of noble birth. But God chose the foolish things of the world to shame the wise; God chose the weak things of the world to shame the strong. God chose the lowly things of this world and the despised things—and the things that are not—to nullify the things that are, so that no one may boast before him. It is because of him that you are in Christ Jesus, who has become for us wisdom from God—that is, our righteousness, holiness and redemption. Therefore, as it is written: "Let the one who boasts boast in the Lord."

(1 Corinthians 1:18–31 NIV)

There are limits to what we can do, and there are no limits with God. And any time, anywhere, we can expect him to intervene in the affairs of men and rescue people from the precipice. Restore broken hearts and bring freshness to those who are without hope. Jesus is the author of life and "the way, the truth, and the life" (John 14:6 ESV). The story of the resurrection of Lazarus is demonstration of God's power and what God can do. And Paul says, "For to me to live is Christ and to die is gain" (Philippians 1:21 ESV). Death becomes subservient to those who have a relationship with Christ. This has implications on the way we view life and all that happens to us. The end is not here but beyond. Death cannot frighten us, as it is not the end but the beginning of life itself. This is difficult to comprehend, but it is important to hold on to it. This is why, before God, the broken pieces of our lives can be reconstituted. They can be put in place again. This is because God is the potter and we are the clay. He has the prerogative over our lives, and all we need to do is to acquiesce and see him do what he does best.

The challenge is how to deal with the unconvinced. How do you deal with those people whose mindset is bent on unbelief and rationality? Those who see a contradiction between the natural and the spiritual who put limits on what God can do. When Lazarus was raised from the dead, the Pharisees reacted angrily. It was impossible for someone dead to rise again. It was impossible for life to come out of nothing. Of course they had forgotten that unless a seed dies, no new life can come from it. They hounded Lazarus. He was a pain because he was evidence of the power of God and what Jesus had done.

> When the large crowd of the Jews learned that Jesus was there, they came, not only on account of him but also to see Lazarus, whom he had raised from the dead. So the chief priests made plans to put Lazarus to death as well.
>
> (John 12:9–10 ESV)

They were so incensed by what Jesus had done that they wanted to get rid of the alibi: Lazarus. Jesus would become popular and many would follow him. Well, when God picks up the broken pieces of your life, he impacts others. Word gets round as you testify to the goodness of God. It is always done for a purpose. We discussed earlier in the book that when God restores you, he does it for a purpose. He wants you to encourage others in similar situations to take heart. You should give hope to the hopeless and faith to the faithless.

Martha said to him, "I know that he will rise again in the resurrection on the last day." Jesus said to her, "I am the resurrection and the life. Whoever believes in me, though he die, yet shall he live."

(John 11:24–25 ESV)

This exudes confidence in all those who are broken. If he is the author of life, then he can bring it back. If he is the author of life, then he can mend it. Period. What a difference this makes to your predicament, to all of our life's challenges. Mary and Martha's strategy was to have hope in their friend. They had faith that if and whenever Jesus hears or sees their problem, he would deal with it. They were convinced he could have prevented it from the start. And the worst-case scenario was that their brother would rise up at the end of life. Little did they know that God was timeless and was capable of doing this anytime, should he so wish. And he did. And so he can. Today. Anytime. The reason is that he is God. And the Bible is awash with stories of men and women who were given life in this world. Ezekiel mentions the case of bones being revived. And of course their DNA intact as it can survive for millions of years.

Then he said to me, "Prophesy to these bones and say to them, 'Dry bones, hear the word of the LORD! This is what the Sovereign LORD says to these bones: I will make breath enter you, and you will come to life. I will attach tendons to you and make flesh come upon you and cover you with skin; I will put breath in you, and you will come to life. Then you will know that I am the LORD.'"

So I prophesied as I was commanded. And as I was prophesying, there was a noise, a rattling sound, and the bones came together, bone to bone. I looked, and tendons and flesh appeared on them and skin covered them, but there was no breath in them.

Then he said to me, "Prophesy to the breath; prophesy, son of man, and say to it, 'This is what the Sovereign LORD says: Come, breath, from the four winds and breathe into these slain, that they may live.'" So I prophesied as he commanded me, and breath entered them; they came to life and stood up on their feet—a vast army.

(Ezekiel 37:4–10 NIV)

Be careful what you call impossible, for with God, all things are possible. He can restore you to your original self. He is God.

Rise up and Walk

You heard it. It is not just rising up. It is walking as well. Jesus was always careful to instruct whoever he healed to take up their mat and walk. They had to physically leave their present state and take a step away from that which was inhibiting them from enjoying a life of freedom and independence.

Psychologically this meant detaching them from that which could potentially hold them from fulfilling their new destiny. If you remain stuck where you are even after you are made well, the temptation is to continue enjoying the environment and never know what is ahead of you. It can cloud your vision and prevent you from seeing that the best is yet to come. The detachment of a baby's umbilical cord heralds the beginning of an independent existence and a breaking with the past. This is why it was important for Jesus to tell those he healed to move on and forget what lies ahead. It involved a step of faith and the ability to launch into the unknown, knowing that he who unshackled them from their present situation would see them through the next hurdle.

> When Jesus came into contact with a man who had been sitting by the pool side for thirty-eight says, this is what the man said, "Sir, I have no one to put me into the pool when the water is stirred up, and while I am going another steps down before me." Jesus said to him, "Get up, take up your bed, and walk." And at once the man was healed, and he took up his bed and walked.
> (John 5:7–9 ESV)

Notice Jesus's methodology. He asks the man to get up first. He had to gather the courage to do what he had not done before. By faith, he focused on Jesus. He responded to an instruction. He had to do it. Do something. Refuse to remain where he had been for thirty-eight years. Wow! The temptation is to sit there. The temptation is to just reminisce. To be nostalgic about what has happened in your life. What happens is that you have a fear of the unknown. You feel pity for yourself. To want to receive sympathy as you have done for many years. When you are broken, the message is loud and clear. "Get up." That is not where you should be. You were not meant to wallow in the quagmire of your circumstances.

And Jesus says something even more practical and difficult. Take up your mat. Get rid of that which was your comfort zone all these years. Remove it and take it on yourself. Get rid of any thoughts of the surroundings from where you experienced your discomfort and pain. Literally take it yourself and move away. Go. Don't hang around. You are free. You have been delivered. This has been done once and for all. It takes an act of courage to look at your challenge and then to walk away.

Don't fall in the trap of being so shackled in body and in spirit by your situation so much that when you are released, you remain where you are. You now don't see any difference from where you are and where you are going. This is what Jesus sought to do. And when the demon-possessed man wanted to hang around Jesus after he was healed, Jesus told him to go and tell others what he had done for him. Whatever you're going through, however much you are hurt and broken, however much you have given up, rise up and walk. Take the first steps and move away from the scene. Don't look back, for there is nothing there. Begin again. Do it today.

Change begins with you. When you start to change, your environment and situation follow suit. How easy it is to blame others, the economy, and your history without focussing on you and what you need to do. When Jesus healed people, he challenged many of the people to do something themselves. To believe, to go and wash, to respond to the miracle. In other words, do something. When we are broken, the tendency is to wallow in our pity and expect sympathy from others. Stand up. Believe in yourself, in a God of the impossible, and go for it. Remember the angels that came to visit Abraham? They made a profound rhetorical question. "Is anything too hard for the Lord?" Individually we have to have that kind of mindset. A recognition that whatever we are going through, there is a way out. A dogged determination to raise ourselves up and do what it takes to bounce back to our normal self. It is hard work. It is determination. It is being focused, dedicated, and committed.

When we are broken, it is not a waiting game. We take the initiative. Remember Jesus told his disciples that they only need the faith of a mustard seed. One of the smallest seeds is shoved into the hostile soil, pounded by incessant storms, but still manages to rise up and become a tree. That is how small our faith has to be. The key is taking the initiative and not taking everything lying down. One step at a time towards the resolution of our situation. The key is to do something consistently.

It is not a waiting game. We take the initiative. God expects us to behave that way. Until we can leap in faith in response to his command, we will remain where we are. We remain stuck in the same situation. It is empowering to know that whatever situation we are going through, the power to get up and go is imbedded in us. It is the very stuff that we are made up of. And God yearns for us to respond to his bidding and go.

On another occasion, Jesus says to another disabled person, "But I want you to know that the Son of Man has authority on earth to forgive sins." So he said to the man, "I tell you, get up, take your mat and go home" (Mark 2:10 NIV).

What a relief this man must have felt. But he had to do something himself. Get up, take his bed, and go home. Jesus recognised the potential of those entire communities he healed. He only facilitated their healing and called upon them to play their part. You must play your part. You may be broken. You may have succumbed to temptation. You are unsure what is going to happen. But you must take the first step. Heave a sigh of relief and stand up. Decide to do something, with God's help. Look ahead and arise. Not easy, but necessary. God beckons you. Come. And you will never be the same again.

When we rise up and walk, it is evidence of what God has done. It demonstrates that we are freed from our situation and it is for all to see. We get out of our cocoons and face the world with confidence.

Chapter 3

If Only I Could Speak

I have worked with people with learning disabilities. And many times I wondered if only they could speak and say they're sorry. Express their wishes and hopes for today and tomorrow. Clarify some of the misconceptions about them. This should include their health, status, communication, hurts, and pain. If only people could just remember that they speak. They have a language. They are aware what goes around them, but sometimes it is difficult to articulate this. And when they do, people refuse to listen, to observe, to be patient, and above all, to listen. Their story is a true story. It comes from the heart. It breeds experience and a life sometimes neglected and shunned because people just don't get it.

God has not robbed them of their imagination. They still have their dreams and hopes. Yet sometimes they are shattered. They lose hope. They are broken. This happens when their parents and relations never turn up. In many cases, they are left on their own, within institutions. Where people try to care and make the environment conducive. Activities are lined up as entertainment. But it is never the same. The experience can be traumatic, especially when your siblings keep at arm's length. When your mum pretends you are but a tourist attraction to be visited during the summer and when they are bored. And only at Christmas one can expect a sing-along from the Salvation Army. And it's for a season. Staff pretend to love, yet deep down, it's only a job for them. It's about how to please the Regulatory authorities. It is all about reports, the supervisions, and the paperwork necessary to ensure compliance with regulations. You get broken. You lose hope, and there seems to be no hope for tomorrow.

How do you get out of this rut? Who will rescue you from all this. Mephibosheth, Saul's son, got the favour of the king. And all his life he was cared for at the palace. He had a meal at the high table in the presence of the king. How fortunate.

While our society tries hard to care for those with mental challenges and learning disabilities, occasionally you will hear stories of people who failed to care. People who abdicated their responsibility and their duty of care. How sad this is. Instead of caring, someone exploits the situation to their selfish ends. Instead of picking up the pieces, they contribute towards the person's downfall. Humanity at its worst. Sad. What a missed opportunity.

One the greatest satisfactions one can have is to be able to say, "I did all I could to help facilitate the empowerment of another individual." To walk with them, to laugh when they laugh, and to experience their frustration when they struggle to communicate. And to respond prosocially when they feel agitated. You see, picking up the pieces calls for a "new way of thinking," a new way of responding, and a bag full of love and generosity. These are endangered characteristics in today's world.

I was privileged to work with a young man who had learning disabilities but showed great wit and intelligence. We would sit and discuss real-life issues: his goals and frustrations. He wanted to marry one day and realised that he needed to have a steady relationship in order to do this. When he did, it was a joy to watch him and his girlfriend share stories, laugh together, and even cook for each other. Occasionally, I would play a love song on my guitar, and before long, I was invited to come to their wedding one day! What an experience I had realising how I could make a difference. How I could walk alongside these two lovebirds deemed "disabled" yet having fun all the way. If this is not picking up the pieces, what is?

You can never be able to facilitate the picking up of someone's pieces, if your attitude is not right. This is one of the greatest challenges facing our society today. We categorise people and immediately write them off if they don't fit into what we term "normal." Whenever I travelled on the bus with someone with mental or learning disability challenges, it was obvious from some people's responses that they were still uncouth when it came to accepting others as people rather than deprived beings. Just the stare was enough for me to get their message. What a contrast to Jesus, who went into the thick and thin of society. Risked his reputation by associating with those on the fringe of society. No wonder why he is such a great big, wonderful God. He sees you as you are. You can interact with him as you are, and there are no specials on his guest list. No VVIP guests either! I am sure that would make some people's stomachs turn! Tough!

What ought to be an opportunity to be actively involved in the empowering and facilitating of one's development ends up negatively influenced by obsolete attitudes that have become a cancer to our society. Instead of picking up the pieces, many end up exploiting vulnerable members of our community. Among them children and the elderly. While God is in the business of picking up the pieces, he uses people to do this. Sadly, many choose to go against the norm and be part of the destructive system that does not see people as people but as mere objects of abuse. Today, children have to be protected even in church, which is supposed to be a place of sanctuary and safety. This is how bad the situation has become. The people that are deemed to be the custodians of children and vulnerable adults have become ferocious wolves preying on them. These include politicians, the clergy, celebrities, and the list goes on. If only vulnerable members of our communities could speak; if only they could be given an opportunity to respond. They are broken and seek an environment where they can come out of their brokenness. Sad.

These are some of the obstacles that many face in their journey towards freedom. As God seeks to pick them up and restore their dignity and humanity. Laws have been instituted against abuse, yet it continues unabated. Regular training by those who work with vulnerable people keep happening, yet even the very parents of children sometimes become the perpetrators of these terrible crimes. We are all responsible and accountable. Unless we are willing to change our attitudes towards those who are vulnerable, it will be difficult to minimise or eliminate this terrible cancer. Unless we are willing to be educated on how to look after other members of our community, we will remain where we are. The initiative has to start with you as an individual. Seek to change, and others will change with you. Seek to help, and others will help with you.

It is difficult to imagine how vulnerable adults feel inside when they go through such abuse. Sitting in a chair all day, transported from bed to lounge to dining room. Eat, sleep, and eat. They must cringe inside. Stare at life with unanswered questions. How long will this last is difficult to imagine. This is what broken means and feels. This is the ultimate in brokenness. You shout for help and no one hears you. What do you hold on to? How can you come out of this shell? Where is the miracle? "Who is in charge of the universe?" you ask. Where is tomorrow? Where is the future? Where will I be, and what will I become? If only I could speak your language, because you don't understand mine. How frustrating.

This is why stories of the blind seeing, the lame walking, and the mentally challenged made whole are gems in the Bible. You can imagine how relieved these people must have felt. After years of being bottled up without recourse to the keys that unlock their access to life as we know it. You can imagine how the man at the gate walked, leaped, and praised God entering the temple. This was no mean feat. It was the beginning of a brand-new world. The original pieces were being put together and life was being enjoyed to the full.

This is the world we are living in, a world we have lived in before. People with learning disabilities are at the mercy of the state and its regulations. They are pawns in a game of cultural intolerance. And like Paul, they cry.

> Wretched man that I am! Who will set me free from the body of this death? Thanks be to God through Jesus Christ our Lord! So then, on the one hand I myself with my mind am serving the law of God, but on the other, with my flesh the law of sin.
>
> (Romans 7:24)

We will never know how God undertakes this salvage operation on people with learning disabilities. How he instils peace, joy, and love in them. How? Or should we be allowed to know? Is it our business? Is it not that just as we are not able to decipher what they say and how they feel that we may not appreciate their bliss when they show it?

I was privileged to assist an elderly lady who had challenging behaviour. It took some time for me to appreciate her and to realise how fulfilled and contented she was in her own way. When she was anxious and agitated, she expressed this in her unique way. She wanted me to know that she was not in a good place. And as I gained experience, I began to respond prosocially. I was able to acknowledge that all she was doing was to show me her inner turmoil that she could not control.

That she was, in effect, crying out for someone to share her inner conflict with her. That it was nothing personal. As time went on, we developed an understanding of each other. She would be raging one minute in her room and, as soon as I walked in, would say, "I didn't know that you were here. How are you?" I cherished those moments of her highs and lows. Moments punctuated by what I could call "normal." But the most memorable and touching encounter I had with her was when her health had deteriorated and she was now in hospital. When I sat by her bed one night, her face lit up and she clutched onto my hand. She stared at me intensely for a while and said, "I am glad you came tonight." When I came back a few days later, she could not speak until she breathed her last two weeks later while I was with her with two other colleagues. She was free at last, but not before she left an impact on me and many of those who interacted with her.

It is a mystery, but God is in the business of picking the pieces of those who are vulnerable living with learning disabilities. All of us should stand ready to be part of God's rescue team in love.

CHAPTER 4

Leave Your Baggage and Move On

We all have baggage in our closets. For some, these are vivid memories of yesteryear. Close-shave encounters where it happened or you almost did it. This includes a broken promise, a lustful relationship, or an unforgiving pal, pastor, friend, brother, or sister. Something rings a bell in your conscience. You wish you could revisit that again and, perhaps, repent, seek forgiveness, and redo. But it's today and not yesterday. That baggage cannot answer today's challenges. It can only make you retrogress and not move on with your life. Your best bet is to move on. You should acknowledge yesterday but hold on to today. You must learn from yesterday but resist control from it. Sometimes you can still have vivid memories of what happened. Keep them as memories. They should lie dormant and not affect the present. The best you can do is deal with them once and for all.

Zacchaeus in the Bible worked for the Department of Taxes and Revenue/Internal Revenue Service. He was an official of the Roman occupiers. He was rich. He was corrupt, until he met Jesus. At dinner with Jesus, he decided to get rid of his baggage; he offered to repay fourfold those people he had taken money from. This was very drastic but liberating. And Jesus made a pronouncement. "Today salvation has come to this house." Zach was free. He had made a decision. He got rid of his baggage. His encounter with Jesus enabled him to deal with his baggage. Restitution was the answer. He found a solution to a problem that had dogged him for a long time. And that was the beginning of a new life. This was a new life of freedom, peace, and progress. You see, it depends how broken you are and what has caused your brokenness. Sometimes you have to accept responsibility before you can move on. Sort out the mess with God's help and then move on.

> The writer to the Hebrews says, "Therefore, since we are surrounded by such a great cloud of witnesses, let us throw off everything that hinders and the sin that so easily entangles. And let us run with perseverance the race marked out for us."
>
> (Hebrews 12:1–2 NIV)

The key is to identify those areas in our broken past that prevent us from moving forward. Face these head on, and deliberately decide to eliminate these before moving on. They are hurdles that make it difficult to do that which God intended for us. They are obstacles on our way. They can frustrate us. They can rob us of our joy and happiness, without which it is impossible to live our lives to the full and to achieve our goals. What has been a hindrance to your progress? What drags you back to yesteryear? Is it worth mulling over? We need to forget the past and focus on the future. It is not easy, but it is worth it. That is where we are going. The past is where we have been, and we cannot go back again. We can only look forward to a new day and not yesterday. So what is holding you? Move on. Now!

What God wants you to remember of yesterday is your benefits, what God has done for you. Count your blessings; name them one by one. They are the stuff that keeps you going. You stay focused and diverted from distractions. Be in the company of those who would always remind you of your successes and not your failures. This lot seems like an endangered species but is worth looking for. This begs the question "Can two walk together except they are in agreement?" (Amos 3:3 KJV). They are like birds of a feather. That's what you are looking for. You may disagree on certain issues, but in the main, you are cut from the same cloth. You are able to challenge one another. Keep your standards high and your goal to be the best you can be. To make your life better so you can be of service to others. Use your past to re-engineer the present. And in the words of the old classic hymn, "It is no secret what God can do. What he has done for others he can do for you. With arms wide open he will pardon you, it is no secret what God can do" (lyrics by Jim Reeves). If others who have been broken are restored, then the same can happen to you, to us, to everyone.

You may have been given a few months or years to live because of a terminal illness. This is the worst in brokenness. But God wants you to look to him in faith. God wants you to look to the future in hope. Holding on to what his Word says. David was in the same predicament and this is how he responded: "My flesh and my heart may fail, but God is the strength of my heart and my portion forever."

And Job said a similar thing.

> As for me, I know that my Redeemer lives, and at the last He will take His stand on the earth. Even after my skin is destroyed, Yet from my flesh I shall see God; Whom I myself shall behold, And whom my eyes will see and not another. My heart faints within me!
>
> (Job 19:25–27 ESV)

And Paul acknowledges the pain and suffering that our bodies go through each day but still hopes in God.

"For while we are still in this tent, we groan, being burdened—not that we would be unclothed, but that we would be further clothed, so that what is mortal may be swallowed up by life" (2 Corinthians 5:4 ESV).

We cannot explain why we go through such tough times. Why our bodies fail us. It is a mystery. Just like we cannot explain how God made us, our intricate parts. And when God tells us to hope in him when we go through such tough times, I guess we ought to take him at his word. "God is not man, that he should lie, or a son of man, that he should change his mind. Has he said, and will he not do it? Or has he spoken, and will he not fulfill it?" (Numbers 232:19 ESV).

The reality is that our bodies are a tent, housing the other parts of us: the spirit and the soul. While the physical body may waste away, we still know that our spirit is being renewed and ultimately will be presented before God intact on the day when we will assume a new body. What a hope.

Now that you are free, why look back? Now that you are delivered, why contemplate about what could have happened? It is the recurrence of negative memories about yesteryear? About what you should not have done? It is one thing to let God pick up the pieces; it is another to continue to dream about the pieces that God has dealt with already.

This is why it is important to select your friends wisely. To hang around those who have deliberately decided to look to tomorrow. To appreciate what has been done. And not to mourn over what was and what could have been. Decide your friends. Decide your literature. Make up your mind what you will allow your eyes to see, your mind to think about, and your environment to embrace. This is because it is about your welfare, about how you move on from now.

Those who have not experienced release—be they friends or fellow Christians—can be toxic. They can influence you back to yesterday. They can dig up the past they knew and not the present you experience. They are comfy discussing judgementally what you used to do and unable to cope with the new you. The you that God has transformed. The you that God will use to change others. You see, wise counsel comes from those who have been through it all. People whose competence is not purely technical but experiential. Those who can say, "I have been through it." The ones who can show you their scars and near misses when they were broken. You ought to welcome this group. Embrace it, and seek to learn from it. As has been mentioned before, you are mended for a purpose, so you can be part of God's process of picking up the pieces. He uses people.

He uses you and every experience. It is part of the equipping that God does time and time again. No need to be negative about what has been, what has happened in your life. You will suffer the consequences but only as part of God's discipline in order to teach you a lesson or lessons for the future. But still don't look back. Refuse to carry the baggage. You are free now. You have work to do. You have an assignment to champion the cause of the one who picked up your pieces in the first place. We are all works in progress. We are all being refined. Just like dross, we go through the refiner's fire. Daily. For our own good. The result is purified gold that is fit for purpose. Something honourable.

> These trials will show that your faith is genuine. It is being tested as fire tests and purifies gold—though your faith is far more precious than mere gold. So when your faith remains strong through many trials, it will bring you much praise and glory and honour on the day when Jesus Christ is revealed to the whole world.
>
> (1 Peter 1:7 NLT)

You can happily leave your baggage behind, because the purpose was to bring out another you—tried and tested through fiery trials. Character and resilience are yours through the experience of yesterday. You don't have to go back there. In fact, you cannot go back. You are in a different world, a different league. It is when we realise how much God has done for us that we want to move on and be of use to others who are still in the same predicament. You regard what has gone before for what it is; baggage that is heavy, cumbersome, and prohibiting. And because we are in a race, it ceases to be useful. You want to be free to run your race with nothing on you.

> But [like a boxer] I buffet my body [handle it roughly, discipline it by hardships] and subdue it, for fear that after proclaiming to others the Gospel *and* things pertaining to it, I myself should become unfit [not stand the test, be unapproved and rejected as a counterfeit.
>
> (1 Corinthians 9:27 AMP)

The task ahead now is rigorous exercise in order to achieve personal discipline and enable us to effectively accomplish what God has assigned for us. It is when we have this attitude that the baggage will be forgotten. You have something to do. You are busy. You are focused on the task at hand. You cannot forget yesterday if you are comfortable in the present. You cannot be productive if you are doing nothing in the present. Like the ants in the book of Proverbs, go on. Work.

> Go to the ant, you sluggard;
> consider its ways and be wise!

It has no commander,

no overseer or ruler,

yet it stores its provisions in summer

and gathers its food at harvest.

(Proverbs 6:6–8 NIV)

You have a job to do. Daily, you plan, prepare, and then execute. You anticipate the risks and you go on full steam ahead to achieve your goals and complete the mission that was God's original intention for your life. Dreams are for tomorrow. Hopes are in the future. The past is in the dustbin of history except for the lessons learned. It is truly gone with the wind! To God be the glory.

Many of us have strugggled with leaving our emotional baggage behind. It seems we can't make it with a light load. We are in the habit of hoarding, intentionally or unintentionally. With baggage, you have to toss it or run the risk of being bogged down and allowing it to bear you down. You have to release the hurt, the pain, and the disappointments of yesterday, however devastating. This will allow you to freely move on, unfettered, to your intended destiny. This will allow you to keep track of your focus.

Yes, move on. Let not your baggage hold you. It is retrogressive and not progressive. It will wear you down and not catapult you to another level.

But all this begs the questions "How do you get rid of the baggage? And what will be the result, in your life and to those around you?" Paul, the great apostle and missionary, answers this.

"Therefore, since we are surrounded by so great a cloud of witnesses, let us also lay aside every weight, and sin which clings so closely, and let us run with endurance the race that is set before us."

(Hebrews 12:1–2 ESV)

Again he takes up the theme in Philippians.

"Not that I have already obtained this or am already perfect, but I press on to make it my own, because Christ Jesus has made me his own. Brothers, I do not consider that I have made it my own. But one thing I do: forgetting what lies behind and straining forward to what lies ahead, I press on toward the goal for the prize of the upward call of God in Christ Jesus."

(Philippians 3:11–14)

You are in a race. You've got to lay down everything that can wear you down. It is a race that you have to win and depends on the goal before you and not on what you accumulated in the past. Many times, that is what we do. We accumulate stuff—useless stuff. And we hinder our progress. Keep reminding ourselves about what happened and miss the opportunities of the day. Move on. Forget the past. Run with anticipation of tomorrow and not yesterday. Go on. Now!

Chapter 5

Leave Your Baggage: Forgive

You remain broken if you remain bitter. You remain bitter if you refuse to forgive. You experience freedom when you love your brother as yourself. There are no shortcuts. You can't hop, skip, and jump life's journey. God didn't. He had to send his own son to suffer and ultimately die so he could deal with the problem of sin. We would have remained estranged from the Creator, were it not for his loving-kindness.

You have to make hard choices to remain imprisoned because of your unforgiveness or to break the chains of bitterness and unforgiveness. Nations have collapsed because of one man's unforgiveness. Nelson Mandela, the former president of South Africa, was jailed for twenty-seven years. When he came out of prison, he had to make a hard choice. Either to forgive or forever remain a prisoner in himself. You see, failure to forgive affects you more than the perpetrator. When you forgive, you experience freedom in yourself and you are able to do far more than when you remain unforgiving. Here is very important advice that can help us get rid of the baggage and move on. Mother Teresa often used this quote:

1. People are illogical, unreasonable, and self-centred.
2. Love them anyway.
3. If you do good, people will accuse you of selfish ulterior motives.
4. Do good anyway.
5. If you are successful, you win false friends and true enemies.
6. Succeed anyway.
7. The good you do today will be forgotten tomorrow.
8. Do good anyway.
9. Honesty and frankness make you vulnerable.
10. Be honest and frank anyway.
11. The biggest men and women with the biggest ideas can be shot down by the smallest men and women with the smallest minds.
12. Think big anyway.
13. People favor underdogs but follow only top dogs.
14. Fight for a few underdogs anyway.
15. What you spend years building may be destroyed overnight.
16. Build anyway.
17. People really need help but may attack you if you do help them.
18. Help people anyway.

19. Give the world the best you have and you'll get kicked in the teeth.
20. Give the world the best you have anyway.

Kent M. Keith (1968, 2001)

Families have stagnated because members held on to what happened in years gone by. Legacies were destroyed because people were sucked into disputes and controversies that they refused to resolve. Husbands and wives deprived their children of scarce quality time for years until it was too late to revisit their lives. All because of unforgiveness. All because one person refused to humble themselves. What a tragedy.

Jesus tells the parable of the man who was forgiven yet was unforgiving himself. This is a classic example of what God expects from us seeing that he has forgiven us and decided to forget what we did in the past. See what lessons you can learn from this parable that Jesus told.

> Then Peter came up and said to him, "Lord, how often will my brother sin against me, and I forgive him? As many as seven times?" Jesus said to him, "I do not say to you seven times, but seventy-seven times."
>
> Therefore the kingdom of heaven may be compared to a king who wished to settle accounts with his servants. When he began to settle, one was brought to him who owed him ten thousand talents. And since he could not pay, his master ordered him to be sold, with his wife and children and all that he had, and

payment to be made. So the servant fell on his knees, imploring him, "Have patience with me, and I will pay you everything." And out of pity for him, the master of that servant released him and forgave him the debt. But when that same servant went out, he found one of his fellow servants who owed him a hundred denarii, and seizing him, he began to choke him, saying, "Pay what you owe." So his fellow servant fell down and pleaded with him, "Have patience with me, and I will pay you." He refused and went and put him in prison until he should pay the debt. When his fellow servants saw what had taken place, they were greatly distressed, and they went and reported to their master all that had taken place. Then his master summoned him and said to him, "You wicked servant! I forgave you all that debt because you pleaded with me. And should not you have had mercy on your fellow servant, as I had mercy on you?" And in anger his master delivered him to the jailers, until he should pay all his debt. So also my heavenly Father will do to every one of you, if you do not forgive your brother from your heart.

(Matthew 18:21–35 ESV)

God takes forgiveness seriously. It is at the heart of his relationship with mankind.

You are never more like God than when you forgive. And you have been forgiven and therefore, because of the forgiveness of God in Christ, you ought to forgive one another, and if you don't forgive one another, then God relationally is going to keep His distance from you and put His hand of chastening on you rather than His hand of blessing.

(John MacArthur, www.gty.org 1991)

Unforgiveness is one of the heaviest bags you can ever carry. And many have faltered along the journey because of their unforgiveness. You cannot move on with freedom without doing forgiveness. The past will haunt you by reminding you of what you have not done. You will find it difficult to fight future battles without clearing your unforgiveness locker. Joseph in Egypt freed himself. And God honoured what he did. He was a force to reckon with. Are you a force to be reckoned with? What stops you? You will be hurt in the future so you need to deliberately plan in anticipation to forgive in *advance*.

The great men and women in our world, past and present, took a cue from Jesus's example. They forgave. Nelson Mandela, after languishing in prison for twenty-seven years, came out not bitter but forgiving. It is clear that he knew if he did not leave his bitterness and hatred behind, he would remain a prisoner. His mindset would continue to be that of a prisoner unable to unshackle himself from the chains of slavery.

Mandela made a deliberate choice. It was a hard choice. To forgive. He had to leave the baggage behind in order to move on to real freedom. Knowing that yesterday had to go, no matter what others thought. And he began his new life standing tall. Respected and admired. That was the price worth paying. And we need to be that mature. This is the essence of Christianity. What a world we would create. And it is possible. Today. Resolve to do so as you finish reading this chapter. You see, if you are not reconciled to your brother or sister, to your workmate or fellow pastor, you are building on the sand. Whatever you do will not last if it cannot stand the test of integrity. It is chaff.

You have been forgiven. God has forgiven you. And now the onus is on you to forgive. "Forgive us our sins, for we also forgive everyone who sins against us. And lead us not into temptation" (Luke 11:4 NIV). We forgive because we have been forgiven. We have no right to be bitter or to hold on to the hurts and pains that have been lumbered on us in the past. We need to make a conscientious decision to get rid of whatever holds us back. It is for our own good. It is therapeutic. It frees the soul. It is a sound investment. It releases the energy to allow us to do greater things. To stay focused, to be proactive, and to look forward. So forget the past and move on.

I experienced a tragedy in my life many years ago. I was hurt, broken, and left in despair. Culturally, in my context, nothing happens by coincidence. It must have a cause. Someone came and said to me that they had caused the tragedy. They were nasty to my family and wanted to make sure my parents too suffered psychologically. I felt bitter, but thank God, I came to my senses. I forgave the person. And at one time, we were sent with that person as part of a delegation to represent the local school board to the council. We made a very good presentation together, and happily, the school benefited. What freedom, what joy. We moved on. And this had a great impact on the community.

Jesus goes beyond this when he calls on us to love our enemies and "Pray for those who persecute us." What? Yes, this is the stuff that makes those who genuinely follow Jesus. When you hate your enemy, you carry baggage. When you can't stand other people, you bear the weight of your actions. It slows you down. You can't grow. You remain where you were: static.

God has forgiven us, big time. David says, "As far as the east is from the west, so far has he removed our transgressions from us" (Psalm 103:12 NIV).

This is drastic. God breaks the link. He remembers our sins no more. Job done, and then he moves on to other things. This is our challenge today, that we forget the past and move on. We must cast our burden and move on. Be it emotional or physical baggage. It is not easy for many of us to get rid of our baggage. One of the ways we can do this is to realise that we too are responsible for that baggage. The responsibility concept transforms you into owning up for your mistakes and taking full responsibility for it. To realise that you have the power to create anew to forge a new path and the ability to clear your baggage closet and start afresh.

Getting rid of your baggage means the end of the blame game. You are not overly concerned about who did what and when but about what you can be tomorrow without that heavy load. Jesus deliberately told the disciples,

> Come to me, all who labor and are heavy laden, and I
> will give you rest. Take my yoke upon you, and learn
> from me, for I am gentle and lowly in heart, and you
> will find rest for your souls. For my yoke is easy, and
> my burden is light.
>
> (Matthew 11:28–30 ESV)

This becomes a routine process if you want to get rid of your baggage. You need someone to take the weight off you and walk alongside you. And Jesus makes this invitation to do just that. Accept the existence of the burden and seek the solution to it. The rest is history.

It is not always easy to forget what happened. A refugee or migrant who on fleeing persecution from their country sees their whole family drown when their boat capsized. A mother learning about the disappearance of a plane in which her husband and only child were. A father witnessing the murder of his wife and child by a deranged gunman in the middle of the night. How does one set aside such baggage? How can one restore their joy and live again? This is the most difficult healing process anyone can go through. Still it has to be done, for the sake of those who have gone and for one's sake. Although this is a cliché, it is true: "Life must go on." Your life, my life, our lives.

If it is to do with someone you have not forgiven, forgive them because it is for your own good. It liberates you and not the other person. It is therapeutic. It cleanses you. If you expect to be forgiven by God and others, you must forgive.

It's hard but it has to be done. It is a baggage not worth carrying.

When you commit yourself to something, you make a deliberate choice. You make your intentions clear. You are consistent. You don't budge. You are focused and stay the course. Deliberately choose to forgive. Don't waver. Keep at it and you will reap the benefits. Today, tomorrow, and forever.

We all have a history. We all have baggage. Some still have it in their closet, but some, the wise ones, have decided to download it into the dustbin of history. Never to be retrieved. Whatever the baggage, God is in the business of dealing with it once and for all. What is it you are clinging on to? Take it where it belongs—in history. Experience the new you. Reflect the new you and live the new you. That is all that matters.

When some people go through tough times, they come out stronger. You hear people say, "I kept looking at my children, and that was all I have." They kept focussed. While they hurt inside, they were grateful that they were alive and the children were alive and healthy. They could start all over again.

Remember you are not alone when you feel broken and hurt. There will still be things you ought to be grateful for. And because you are alive, you can begin again.

Yes, the key is starting again. And you can. It requires effort, discipline, and a focused mindset. And with God on your side, nothing is impossible. It is an experience wrapped in a myriad of lessons for you and for posterity—for life.

The story in the Bible of a man possessed by demons and living in tombs is classic. He resembled Mr Iron Man of today.

Tie him with chains, and he would shake them off like pieces of floss. He never left the tombs, until Jesus showed up. He was seen sitting under Jesus's feet and "in his right mind." Complete transformation! A good example of what Jesus was good at. Restoring, making whole, and transforming people. Like a jigsaw puzzle, picking up the pieces one by one and restoring God's creation to its original form.

Imagine if this were company policy across the globe. When people mess up, there would be a department responsible for making good the hurt and pain that were felt. Restoring to his or her original position whoever did cause the hurt and pain. Whatever you are going through, here is an opportunity to begin again. An opportunity to leave yesterday and cleave to tomorrow. And with your baggage behind or under control, you can truly move on.

CHAPTER 6

You Can Cry if You Want to

When the rubber hits the road, you cry. Not prompted but spontaneous. It matters not whether you are male or female, young or old. And it's OK. When you are broken, you know it. And sometimes it's uncontrollable. It is therapeutic. It is a safe valve. This is part of grieving. This sends a signal to the brain that it's tough but it's OK. The coping mechanism is built into the crying mechanism.

You are on the mend when you do it. Moses cried, and so did Nehemiah, Daniel, and Hannah. And Jesus cried when his friend Lazarus died. It's not a woman thing or a man thing or a baby thing. It is the thing. The opposite is disaster. You bottle up and wait for an explosion. You retreat and suffer the consequences of isolation and ultimately you break down.

Yes, when you are broken, you can cry if you want to. God hears the cry of his people. And that is when he intervenes in the affairs of men. He knows you are broken, but when you articulate it, when you mouth it before him, it seems to move him instantly.

He said also, "I am the God of your father, the God of Abraham, the God of Isaac, and the God of Jacob." Then Moses hid his face, for he was afraid to look at God. The Lord said, "I have surely seen the affliction of My people who are in Egypt, and have given heed to their cry because of their taskmasters, for I am aware of their sufferings." So I have come down to deliver them from the power of the Egyptians, and to bring them up from that land to a good and spacious land, to a land flowing with milk and honey, to the place of the Canaanite and the Hittite and the Amorite and the Perizzite and the Hivite and the Jebusite.

(Exodus 3:6–8 NASB)

This was God's response to the people of Israel. And after 430 years, he led them out of Egypt to the Promised Land. He heard their cry and was determined to do something about it. What is it about crying that unlocks the divine and ushers in answers to challenges? Why is crying so effective to the hearer and the one who does the crying? It irritates, it unsettles, and it makes you want to resolve the cause for it. For a parent, it may be succumbing to the request of the child. It moves people. It destabilises people. It starts a chain reaction in attempts to want to resolve the problem.

Throughout history, believers have cried out to God in times of distress. Sometimes after years of praying, a single cry brings direction or deliverance instantly. Many have wondered why there are such powerful results from simply crying out to God, yet the promise is clear. *"Call upon me in the day of trouble: I will deliver you,* and you will honour me" (Psalm 50:15; emphasis mine) NIV

Throughout Scripture, believers are instructed to cry out to God in times of trouble. Here are a few examples:

- "Call unto me, and I will answer thee, and show thee great and mighty things, which thou knowest not" (Jeremiah 33:3 KJV)
- "When the righteous cry for help, the Lord hears and delivers them out of all their troubles" (Psalm 34:17 ESV)
- "Then my enemies will turn back in the day when I call. This I know, that God is for me" (Psalm 56:9 ESV)

Crying out in Scripture

The Bible captures various forms of crying before God that demonstrate the intensity and seriousness of the cry.

A Cry of Deep Distress

"You saw the suffering of our ancestors in Egypt; you heard their cry at the Red Sea. You sent signs and wonders against Pharaoh, against all his officials and all the people of his land, for you knew how arrogantly the Egyptians treated them. You made a name for yourself, which remains to this day. You divided the sea before them, so that they passed through it on dry ground, but you hurled their pursuers into the depths, like a stone into mighty waters."

(Nehemiah 9:9–11 NIV)

To Cry out for Help

When the Israelites could not find fresh water in the wilderness, Moses "cried unto the Lord; and the Lord showed him a tree, which when he had cast into the waters, the waters were made sweet" (Exodus 15:25 NIV).

To Call with a Loud Sound

Jabez called upon the God of Israel, saying, "Oh that you would bless me and enlarge my border, and that your hand might be with me, and that you would keep me from harm so that it might not bring me pain!". And God granted what he asked (1 Chronicles 4:10 ESV)

To Shout a War Cry

"Then the men of Judah gave a shout *[rowan]:* and as the men of Judah shouted it came to pass, that God smote Jeroboam and all Israel" (2 Chronicles 13:15 NIV).

A Cry for Help

"He will fulfil the desire of them that fear him: he also will hear their cry *[shavah]*, and will save them" (Psalm 145:19 NIV).

A Cry of Deep Distress

"He forgetteth not the cry of the humble" (Psalm 9:12).

To Cry Out

When the apostle Peter walked out on the water at the invitation of Jesus, Peter was "afraid; and beginning to sink, he cried *[krazo]*, saying, Lord, save me. Matthew says, "And immediately Jesus stretched forth his hand, and caught *him*" (Matthew 14:30–31 NIV).

To Implore with Strong Voice

A blind man in Jericho heard that Jesus was passing near him. "And he cried *[boao]*, saying, Jesus, thou son of David, have mercy on me … And Jesus said unto him, Receive thy sight: thy faith hath saved thee" (Luke 18:38–42 NIV).

Crying out to God is an act of desperation and total concentration. It is a fervent expression of faith in God and trust in his goodness and power to act on your behalf. Crying out to God expresses the following traits:

- **Genuine Humility**
  It is hard for people to admit that they cannot solve a problem or overcome an obstacle, but it is true that we need God's help. He delights in a broken and contrite heart that humbly seeks his aid. "For he who avenges blood remembers; he does not ignore the cries of the afflicted" (Psalm 9:12; see also Psalm 10:17 NIV).

- **Unconditional Surrender**
  When a situation becomes so desperate that only God can deliver you, a cry represents total, unconditional surrender. Don't try to bargain with God; leave your life in his hands. "If I regard iniquity in my heart, the Lord will not hear me" (Psalm 66:18 KJV).

- **A Plea for Mercy**
  Apart from Christ, we have no value that merits God's favour. When driven to a point of despair or destruction, your unworthiness before God often becomes more apparent, and it can motivate you to cry out to him for mercy. "It is of the Lord's mercies that we are not consumed, because his compassions fail not. They are new every morning: great is thy faithfulness" (Lamentations 3:22–23 KJV).

- **Personal Helplessness**

  Do you tend to believe that you need God's help with only the really hard things? Remember Jesus said, "Without me ye can do nothing" (John 15:5 KJV).

- **Faith in God's Power and Resources**

  Your cry to God acknowledges God's ability to do what no one else can do. During the storm on the Sea of Galilee, the disciples acknowledged Jesus's power to rescue them when they cried out, "Lord, save us: we perish" (Matthew 8:25 KJV).

- **Desperation**

  Crying out to God is an admission of one's need for God. The psalmist declared, "In my distress I called upon the Lord, and cried unto my God: he heard my voice out of his temple, and my cry came before him, even into his ears" (Psalm 18:6 KJV).

And when you are broken, you cry because you are desperate. You want help, and it's fine. And it is during these moments that God comes into his own. He hears. He intervenes. He takes control. Here is how:

Examples of God's Response to Crying Out

The Bible is filled with times when God answered the cries of his people. Below are a few examples of occasions on which individuals cried out to God and God heard their cries and delivered them.

Elijah cried out, and God revived a dead child.

"He cried unto the Lord and said, O Lord my God, hast thou also brought evil upon the widow with whom I sojourn, by slaying her son? And he stretched himself upon the child three times, and cried unto the Lord, and said, O Lord my God, I pray thee, let this child's soul come into him again. And the Lord heard the voice of Elijah; and the soul of the child came into him again, and he revived."

(1 Kings 17:20–22 KJV)

Jehoshaphat cried out, and God delivered him from death.

It came to pass, when the captains of the chariots saw Jehoshaphat, that they said, It is the king of Israel. Therefore they compassed about him to fight: but Jehoshaphat cried out, and the Lord helped him; and God moved them to depart from him.

(2 Chronicles 18:31 KJV)

Hezekiah cried out, and God gave him victory.

Hezekiah the king, and the prophet Isaiah the son of Amoz, prayed and cried to heaven. And the Lord sent an angel, which cut off all the mighty men of valour, and the leaders and captains in the camp of the king of Assyria. So he returned with shame of face to his own land.

(2 Chronicles 32:20–21 KJV)

Jesus's disciples cried out to him in a storm, and Jesus calmed the sea.

As they sailed he fell asleep: and there came down a storm of wind on the lake; and they were filled with water, and were in jeopardy. And they came to him, and awoke him, saying, Master, master, we perish. Then he arose, and rebuked the wind and the raging of the water: and they ceased, and there was calm.

(Luke 8:23–24 KJV)

Blind Bartimaeus called to Jesus, and he restored his sight.

And they came to Jericho. And as he was leaving Jericho with his disciples and a great crowd, Bartimaeus, a blind beggar, the son of Timaeus, was sitting by the roadside. And when he heard that it was Jesus of Nazareth, he began to cry out and say, "Jesus, Son of David, have mercy on me!" And many rebuked him, telling him to be silent. But he cried out all the more, "Son of David, have mercy on me!" And Jesus stopped and said, "Call him." And they called the blind man, saying to him,

"Take heart. Get up; he is calling you." And throwing off his cloak, he sprang up and came to Jesus. And Jesus said to him, "What do you want me to do for you?" And the blind man said to him, "Rabbi, let me recover my sight." And Jesus said to him, "Go your way; your faith has made you well." Immediately he recovered his sight and followed him on the way.

(Mark 10:46 ESV)

Psalm 50:15 declares this word from the Lord: "Call upon me in the day of trouble: I will deliver thee." As children of the living God, our heavenly Father appeals to us to cry out to him for deliverance. Let us be quick to cry out to him with humility, sincerity, and faith. God "will fulfil the desire of them that fear him: he also will hear their cry, and will save them" (Psalm 145:19 KJV).

You are on the right track. When it seems there is nowhere to turn to and no one to confide in, God has opened the doors to himself through the simple act of crying. It is when you are weak that you are strong. When you acknowledge your problem and seek help, you are on the road to recovery. There is nothing girlish about crying. It is the stuff that heroes of the faith used in order to sustain them and get them out of their trouble. It was recognition that without God's help they could do nothing. What a contrast to today's so-called leaders. They are considered strong when there is little or no emotion in them. Any appearance of emotion is a sign of weakness and an inability to cope with the rigours of life.

If Jesus cried, surely anyone in dire straits can and should cry. You can cry if you want to. And God will turn your brokenness into strength.

> Because of wickedness, cast them forth, in anger put down the peoples, O God! "You have taken account of my wanderings; Put my tears in your bottle. Are they not in your book? Then my enemies will turn back in the day when I call; This I know, that God is for Me."
>
> (Psalm 56:8 KJV)

It's amazing how God keeps a record of our tears. He deems them an important indicator of how serious we are and how much we are desperate to resolve our challenges. I remember the last time I cried buckets in a work situation. Relationships had turned sour with my boss and she had set a deadline. I detected a bit of jealousy because of certain responsibilities that I had been given that seemed to deprive her of her authority. I had just finished work. And before I left the office, I suddenly confronted God about it. This turned into a wailing prayer where I literally shed buckets of tears while screaming to God for him to intervene. When I left the office, I felt the burden had gone and I was convinced my God heard me. A few months later, this mountain was removed and she ended up seeking my counsel when she lost the job she had applied for within the organisation.

Chapter 7

Parental Chaos

Parenting has become to many a nightmare. It is the nature of the world we are living in. More so if you are in an unfamiliar environment or culture, which means that what your children learn from outside is not in tandem with what you were taught yourself. A tale of two cultures. The majority of us have taken parenting as a part-time job without considering the long-term effects of a proper lack of preparation for it. By the time many realise this, they are either on medication for depression or they have already attempted suicide. This is where God's competence and instruction come handy. In many cases, God is at the receiving end, mopping up the terrible results of families torn apart because of lack of knowledge on how to deal with their families.

God has always been proactive in whatever he does. He wants to prevent the fires instead of fighting them. So from the beginning, he taught the children of Israel about family management. And the core of this was that teaching started at a very early stage. The first responsibility was for the parents to love the Lord with all their hearts and all their souls and all their strengths and to teach their children the Word of God consistently.

> Now this is the commandment—the statutes and the rules—that the LORD your God commanded me to teach you, that you may do them in the land to which you are going over, to possess it, that you may fear the LORD your God, you and your son and your son's son, by keeping all his statutes and his commandments, which I command you, all the days of your life, and that your days may be long. Hear therefore, O Israel, and be careful to do them, that it may go well with you, and that you may multiply greatly, as the LORD, the God of your fathers, has promised you, in a land flowing with milk and honey.
>
> Hear, O Israel: The LORD our God, the LORD is one. You shall love the LORD your God with all your heart and with all your soul and with all your might. And these words that I command you today shall be on your heart. You shall teach them diligently to your children, and shall talk of them when you sit in your house, and when you walk by the way, and when you lie down, and when you rise. You shall bind them as a sign on your hand, and they shall be as frontlets between your eyes. You shall write them on the doorposts of your house and on your gates.
>
> (Deuteronomy 6:1–9 ESV)

You can trace the cause of parental chaos from two fronts: families not loving God or children not being taught how to live life as God instructed. It is not so easy. There is no magic wand. All what one needs to do is to teach from an early age. To be consistent. To have time to reflect and discuss with your children or parents and to realise that as a unit you need one another.

The Diaspora has been inundated with families that have come here for the first time. People desperate to make a living. Some left very lucrative jobs in search of a new life. Families were sacrificed for the sake of earning that little bit of extra cash. Not quite the American dream but a dream nevertheless. The decision to do this was sometimes made through peer pressure, thoughtful prayers, and in many cases in a huff. Sometimes very little time was given to reflecting on the long-term consequences of these life-changing decisions.

And that has been the issue. Families, husbands, wives, sons, and daughters. Chaotic scenes. Chaotic relationships. Culture shock and overturning of moral absolutes. Nancy's story demonstrates this clearly.

God has no favourites and is no respecter of persons. He is a loving God. He gathers where others scatter. Builds where others destroy. Restores. Forgives. And forgets.

Consider Jessica (imaginary name). She arrived in the United Kingdom penniless. Her dream was fulfilled. At last, life was beginning to make sense. She remembered her mum's advice. Bad company ruins good morals. Now in London, what a place to test her mother's advice.

Three months later, she was pregnant, homeless, and abandoned.

As she walked into the church a year later, she felt transparent. It seemed like every one was blaming her.

The song "What a Friend We Have in Jesus" rang from every corner of the church. She sobbed. She cleared her throat as she sat tucked at the back of the packed church. The baby started to cry. A few people across the aisle stared in her direction. "And the father when he saw his son from a distance, welcomed him with open arms." The pastor concluded the parable of the prodigal son. She started crying. The baby's cry was muzzled. She stood up, looked around, and began walking to the front. "Here is God's love. It is when we think that we have messed up and there is no hope that he says, "Come as you are." She was hysterical. Throwing herself at the feet of the pastor, she screamed, "It's me! It's me!" "Pray for me please"

Old and young streamed to the front. The pianist stopped. There was an eerie silence. It is true. God is in the business of picking up the pieces.

They were no longer pieces but lives made whole. Instantly.

This is just one example of the consequences of one's decision to leave the comfort of one's home and culture and dare to risk the unknown. We have all been glued to our television sets or listened to stories about migrants leaving in their thousands to seek refuge in Europe. Many leave countries embroiled in conflict and arrive at their destination with nothing. People from many faiths. And many not able to make it and dying along the way. Families torn apart, careers destroyed.

This is a great challenge today among Christians who are spiritually neutral but who share a similar culture. As a solution, "home" churches have been established to make people feel at home spiritually. They sing the same songs, speak the same language, and are among familiar surroundings although still in a strange land. Children are groomed to behave as they would back home, even though their environment for the rest of the day is alien. New habits, new acquaintances, and new tastes all compete for the same soul. Parents are under pressure working shifts that defy culture. All night shifts. Little time for family and reflection. Children are left exposed to the spiritual and cultural elements in a foreign environment. You either adapt or die an unpleasant choice—but a necessary choice. A recipe for chaos and confusion. Unintended but born out of a simple decision to be or not to be in the Diaspora.

As if this was not enough, marriage looms on the horizon. Relationships have to be forged and young men and women cry as they don't seem to connect with kith and kin. In fact there are no kith and kin anymore. The new kith and kin are from the global, multicoloured, culturally robust village and not the village boy next door. A crisis of all sorts. Torn between two worlds. Christian guys and girls have become an endangered species. Some pretend and are just like predators waiting to pounce on the next available prey and dump it. Genuine, long-term committed individuals take time to identify. And in this fast-moving and instant world, ties require the patience of God to meet Mr Right or Mrs Right. There are few forums where these life-threatening challenges can be discussed. The church service is one hour; the home is deserted as people scramble for shifts. Communication is zilch as the television, mobile, and other social media possess people. Things matter more than people. It is a crazy situation. It is chaotic. Meanwhile, many fall by the wayside. Husbands are unfaithful, pastors succumb to the lust of the flesh, and young men and women cohabit. The spirit of defiance rules as parents struggle to make their children toe the line.

Many families are broken as a result of being thrust into cross-cultural situations that they have not been prepared for. And for many children, it is the beginning of an identity crisis that, if not addressed, will lead to other social behaviours that parents cannot cope with. Globalisation has meant that the world is now a village next door. Across Europe, the United States of America, and many parts of the world, there continues to be movement of people. Cultural and religious barriers are being broken, and for many families, it is survival under these circumstances that has become a challenge. How do you raise a family outside your cultural context, and how does a child assimilate to the new culture without their culture being bruised?

"Who will marry me?" is the cry from young men and women stuck in the Diaspora through their parents' decisions. Some end up broken. Many make the wrong choices.

Yet in such situations, God remains God. He is still in the business of picking up the broken pieces of people's lives, be they in their culture or aliens elsewhere. He creates platforms where people can be healed, restored, and forgiven. You can still find pockets of spiritual sanity—men and women of integrity who can be reservoirs of spiritual resourcefulness.

God dealt with this dilemma when the children of Israel were on their way to the Promised Land. In Genesis 7:10, he comes up with the blueprint.

> Hear, O Israel: The LORD our God, the LORD is one. Love the LORD your God with all your heart and with all your soul and with all your strength. These commandments that I give you today are to be on your hearts. Impress them on your children. Talk about them when you sit at home and when you walk along the road, when you lie down and when you get up. Tie them as symbols on your hands and bind them on your foreheads. Write them on the doorframes of your houses and on your gates.

It begins in the home, wherever you are. The curriculum or the syllabus is developed and taught in the home. This is passed on throughout the generations. It is not an afterthought. It is fire prevention and not fire fighting. The teaching is proactive rather than reactive. It is deliberate and intentional and not impulsive and by the whim reaction. It is planned and processed and reflective and communicable. Always.

CHAPTER 8

The Nature of God

God is in the business of picking up the pieces because he is qualified to do so. He is competent. That is his core business. That is why he is called the Beginning and the End, the Creator. This is important for us to know that the One we can trust has been in the business before the creation of the world and that this is something he does best. You can rely on him. Every day. His track record is there for everyone to see.

So what is the evidence? He is the Creator. The world was created out of nothing. He brings to be that which does not exist. He created the universe, and he created us in his own image. When man sinned, he lost his relationship with God and was banished from God's presence. But he is not only the Creator. He also restores. When we messed up that relationship, God is the one who decided to restore the relationship through buying back mankind from the Enemy. Man's image was shattered. He was doomed to oblivion. But because of who God is, he put into motion his recovery process. And when God identified with humankind in the form of Jesus Christ, God was in Christ reconciling man to himself. So Jesus suffered, taking the form of a servant in order to reclaim us back to him. God is the solution, and he has done this from the beginning and will continue to do this until the end.

It is therefore important to grasp the nature of this God whose business is picking up the pieces. He does this well, and he does this again and again and again.

God is the provider. He has provided for his people over the ages. And whatever you lack and need to replenish your emotional, physical, and psychological stocks, you are covered. Abraham was asked to do the impossible: sacrifice his own son. By faith, he decided to do it, but just in the nick of time, God decided to honour his faith and provide him with a different sacrifice, thereby sparing his son. The story of the journey from Egypt to Canaan undertaken by the Jews is an incredible demonstration of God's competence when it comes to providing for needs of a desperate people. The fact that they were sometimes not grateful is neither here nor there. But it is recorded that when they were hungry, they were given food in the form of manna. When they were thirsty, water gushed out of rocks. What a God!

God is our Father who is in heaven. It can never get better than this. This means he cares and is not bound by time, space, or location. As one poet said, "In him we live and move and have our being." He is unlimited. And because he is *our* father, we are the apple of his eye. He is jealous and takes special care and attention to what happens to us on a daily basis. He watches over us and cares for us. David says,

"I lift up my eyes to the hills.
From where does my help come?
My help comes from the LORD,
who made heaven and earth.
He will not let your foot be moved;
he who keeps you will not slumber.
Behold, he who keeps Israel
will neither slumber nor sleep.
The LORD is your keeper;
the LORD is your shade on your right hand.
The sun shall not strike you by day,
nor the moon by night.
The LORD will keep you from all evil;
he will keep your life.
The LORD will keep
your going out and your coming in
from this time forth and forevermore."

(Psalm 121 ESV)

Before we were born, he knew all about us. He was involved in the making of the most intricate parts of our bodies.

For you formed my inward parts;
you knitted me together in my mother's womb.
I praise you, for I am fearfully and wonderfully made.
Wonderful are your works;
my soul knows it very well.
My frame was not hidden from you,

> when I was being made in secret,
> intricately woven in the depths of the earth.
> Your eyes saw my unformed substance;
> in your book were written, every one of them,
> the days that were formed for me,
> when as yet there was none of them.
>
> (Psalm 139:11–16 ESV)

So whatever happens to us is of great concern to him. And this means when we are hurt, in pain, or distraught, he takes special interest in our plight. When we mess up, he stands ready to welcome us back to himself as soon as we acknowledge our wrong. He does not treat us as we deserve, because he knows our frailty.

> He will not always accuse,
> nor will he harbour his anger forever;
> he does not treat us as our sins deserve
> or repay us according to our iniquities.
> For as high as the heavens are above the earth,
> so great is his love for those who fear him;
> as far as the east is from the west,
> so far has he removed our transgressions from us.
> As a father has compassion on his children,
> so the LORD has compassion on those who fear him;
> for he knows how we are formed,
> he remembers that we are dust.
>
> (Psalm 103:9–14 NIV)

This gives us hope and confidence, just like the many men and women in the Bible and elsewhere that have put their trust in him. And the result? They were all restored to their original position. And not only that, he holds nothing against us. His love is overwhelming. He is love. And this love is unconditional. He loved us even when we were unlovable, in our most despicable state. This love is his prerogative. It knows no bounds, from the cool and simple to the most outrageous and horrible person there is. From the drug addict to the ladies of the night, from the child sexual abuser to the perverted priest, from the thief to the gays and lesbians, from the murderer to the saint. God is love, and he does this for everybody. He is in the forgiving business. That is why he is able to pick up the broken pieces of our lives. It is no big deal for him because it is his nature. He does it all the time.

Grace and favour aptly sum up the reason why God is qualified to pick us up when we are broken. Grace means unmerited favour. Something good done to us without us deserving it. A windfall of blessings on your life, even when you really feel you are not worthy to receive it. No wonder why Jesus taught his disciples to love their enemies. What? My enemies? Yes. In God's currency, no one escapes the grace of God. Not even the terrorists! Wow! This is the nature, character, and competence of the God whose core business is picking up the broken pieces of people's lives. When God decides, he just picks you. No asking. He just does it. What a contrast to how we do business.

He is the father. He is all present. He is all loving, and he is all knowing. He is faithful, and he has been like that throughout the ages. His love is unconditional. It is one-way love. He is just and true. This is why you can rely on him. He never wavers. He is consistent. Whatever he says, he will do. But he does not overlook evil. He deals with those who go against what he has instructed, but in love. The story of the Prodigal Son demonstrates clearly the kind of Father God is. He is the same, yesterday today, and forever. He does not change. He forgives and is patient with his children. Reading the story of the children of Israel, the Jews, it is clear that God from the beginning displayed his unique characteristics. The Jews were fickle. They changed from one day to the other. They never got satisfied. They easily forgot what God had done for them. Nevertheless, God was patient, he persisted, he was loving, and he never discarded them for the sake of his name. Although from time to time he punished them, he brought them back to himself. What love, what faithfulness, and what patience.

This is why, when you are broken, you can rely on this God who is your Father. You are sure that he will understand what you are going through and will tenderly and lovingly guide you to the place where you feel more confident and at peace with yourself.

God is faithful. He keeps his promises, however long it takes. After 430 years, the children of Israel left Egypt on their way to Canaan as God had promised. It is recorded that it was on the very day that God had appointed. No sooner, no later. You can hardly find people today who are as faithful. This means that you can trust him in your brokenness. You can hold on to him while knowing he will do what he says. You can cast your burdens unto him because he has promised to take care of you. In a world where people have become unreliable, we can count on a faithful God. In a world where people cheat on each other and don't mean what they say, we can look up to the Creator of the universe.

God is just, and that means he is fair. He is an activist fighting for the rights of the downtrodden. He has done so throughout the ages. He is the defender of the oppressed, of the widow, of the orphan, and of those despised by society.

> God, who lives in his sacred Temple,
> cares for orphans and protects widows.
> He gives the lonely a home to live in
> and leads prisoners out into happy freedom,
> but rebels will have to live in a desolate land.
>
> (Psalm 68:5–6 NIV)

Over the ages, God has been the inspiration to many men and women who have championed the cause of the marginalised and the oppressed. People like Mother Teresa, General Booth of the Salvation Army, and many others.

Jesus gave the disciples a sneak preview of how God can be accessed when they asked him to teach them how to pray. This was a lesson in basic communication—the vital ingredients. This clearly shows who God is and how we should approach him. An understanding of who he is and what makes him tick helps resolve many issues—broken issues. A realisation of who he is has an impact on our response to the challenges we face in life. When we are broken, we know we can be made whole again because of who God is.

God is our Father. That immediately changes the dynamics. Jesus loves, he cares, he disciplines, he is merciful, and the list goes on. He is not like any father we have seen. He is powerful, yet he cares; he is the Creator of the universe, yet he communicates with mere mortals. His love is unrivalled. It is unconditional. This is why, in the history of the Jewish nation, he remains consistent. They turned away from him myriad times, yet he still says, "Israel I loved." His love is depicted in the parable of the lost son. The father in the story remained hopeful that his son would one day come back. And he did. To the sound of music, feasting, and demonstration of a love that would never let him go. No wonder why the older son, who remained at home, didn't get it.

This is the Father who is in the business of picking up the pieces of our broken lives. He is qualified and competent to rescue us when we are done. We can have confidence in him. He is reliable. He is tender and will go to great lengths to salvage our lives, however much we destroy ourselves or others do so. His domain is in heaven. That is his citadel. That is where he operates from. He is a deity. He is the supernatural. He was there before the beginning of the world.

A quick look at his names reveals how he is equipped to deal with us no matter how we are deep in trouble. He is Jehovah Rafah, the great healer. Even in times when we cannot see a way out, he remains resolute. He wants to heal us. He is the provider, he is the Almighty. He is the deliverer. He confronts any forces that seek our downfall because we are the apple of his eye. Throughout history, God the Father has demonstrated how good he is, how merciful, kind, patient, and able to deal with us frail human beings.

Even those that do not fully acknowledge him come to his defence when people doubt his capability and his greatness. Job got it rough. He was skinned alive. His wife wanted him to curse God. Job stood his ground, because he knew God would come to his rescue, and he did. Not Job's friends. He was repaid twofold. In the end, he was richer than before. God picked him up. It was his prerogative. What a mighty God. He is always there to help in times of trouble.

It is the acknowledgement of who God is that keeps us on solid ground. It removes doubt from us and keeps our hopes alive. God remains the King in charge of his domain. He never relinquishes his responsibility, however much we mess with his creation. He is the forgiver, the one to be worshipped, the beginning and the end. He is the Creator of time, and he stops time.

CHAPTER 9

You Are Restored for a Purpose

You can never be the same again. In fact, you cannot go home again. Not the same as you were before the salvaging. You are different. You have learned, and you are ready to impart it to others. God sees the end from the beginning. He knows your potential and is ready to let you loose after the experience so you can help others along the way. Ideally, prisoners, after serving time in prison, are expected to change through rehabilitation. Sadly, many don't. It requires a relationship with someone who can mentor them back to life.

Prison experience is supposed to serve as a launching pad for a transformed life that can impact on others.

I was restored for a purpose. To make a difference to all I meet. He wants me to use the rest of my time on this planet wisely. It is a race against time. As Ephesians 4:12 says, "Redeeming the times for the days are evil." I realise now what I did not realise then: that time is the most precious resource at my disposal. Use it wisely. Conserve it, preserve it, and guard it.

"But I have pleaded in prayer for you, Simon that your faith should not fail. So when you have repented and turned to me again, strengthen your brothers" (Luke 22:32 NLT). We can only strengthen others if we ourselves have gone through certain experiences. The motivation and inspiration to do something for others comes from a deep vein of experiences that prompt us to help, to be there when we are needed.

"I will restore to you the years that the swarming locust has eaten, the hopper, the destroyer, and the cutter, my great army, which I sent among you" (Joel 2:25 ESV).

God can restore you to your former glory. He is in the restoration business. He recovers systems that have been broken down completely. When the children of Israel disobeyed God and were destined for destruction, God promised to bring them to their former glory. Israel was going to be reconstituted. And in 1948, the nation of Israel was born. This was the birthing of a new and dynamic people whose skills and talents changed the world. Jewish inventions and entrepreneurship is known across the world. You can be restored too. Yes, you. I can be restored.

Restoration is a process and the following verses provide the evidence. This process is therapeutic.

> "For I will restore health to you, and your wounds I will heal, declares the Lord, because they have called you an outcast: 'It is Zion, for whom no one cares!'"
>
> (Jeremiah 30:17 ESV)

> "I will restore to you the years that the swarming locust has eaten, the hopper, the destroyer, and the cutter, my great army, which I sent among you. You shall eat in

plenty and be satisfied, and praise the name of the Lord your God, who has dealt wondrously with you. And my people shall never again be put to shame."

(Joel 2:25–26 ESV)

"Restore to me the joy of your salvation, and uphold me with a willing spirit."

Psalm 51:12 ESV)

"Repent therefore, and turn again, that your sins may be blotted out, that times of refreshing may come from the presence of the Lord, and that he may send the Christ appointed for you, Jesus, whom heaven must receive until the time for restoring all the things about which God spoke by the mouth of his holy prophets long ago."

(Acts 3:19–21 ESV)

"Instead of your shame there shall be a double portion; instead of dishonour they shall rejoice in their lot; therefore in their land they shall possess a double portion; they shall have everlasting joy."

(Isaiah 61:7 ESV)

"And the Lord restored the fortunes of Job, when he had prayed for his friends. And the Lord gave Job twice as much as he had before."

(Job 42:10 ESV)

God can put the jigsaw puzzles together. It can be messy, slow, and painstaking, but he does it well. All you need to do is to be patient and have hope in God as he begins to deal with the areas of your life that need to be restored.

Sometimes during the process, the pieces don't hold together. It happens all the time. You know you are getting there, but somehow the puzzle falls off. You cannot hold the pieces together. It is the right time to cry for help. This is a time to confide in someone and to acknowledge that you are vulnerable. Support is now required, for no man is an island.

This is the key. We live in isolation. One television, one laptop, one iPhone, and sometimes in a strange environment. And it bottles up when it is not shared. When it bursts, it may be too late. You are wiser than that. You love life and you have been promised life in its abundance. So whether the pieces hold together or not, you are in control because God is covering your back.

Can you identify the pieces in your life that don't hold together? This may be an unfaithful husband or wife or a relationship that has gone adrift for years. Each time you think about it, it brings back heart-breaking memories. Some of these issues go back many years and still remain unresolved. What you treasure most is resolution of relationships in accordance with what God says in his Word. You are still on a journey to heaven and the requirements are that you have a clean heart and a track record second to none.

You hear stories of people who fell out with their parents or their siblings. It sounds grand at the time. The reasons may be genuine, and in due course, they come back. One of the greatest challenges facing parents is their children going wayward and wondering whether God will ever be able to bring them back.

One of the greatest qualities of God as a Father is that he never gives up on his children. This is why we can say with confidence that, whatever situation you are in, you can be restored. Jesus tells the story of the parable of the Prodigal son. The young man decided to ask for what was due to him and left home. However, when the going got tough and he ended up feeding from pigs' food, he came to his senses and decided to go back home. When he got there, his father was waiting and received him warmly to the amazement of his brother who had remained at home. This story captures the essence of who God is, what ideal fatherhood means, and how even errant sons and daughters like us can come back "home" and expect royal treatment. It sounds too good to be true, but this is the nature of God and this is what we should emulate if we are to make this world a different place to live.

Many parents struggle with their errant sons and daughters. Like the Prodigal Son, they have left home and lived like they were never taught how to live. My mother used to have a slogan that went, "Bad company ruins good morals." It was her mantra all the time. Her concern was that I should walk in the ways of God and not get sucked up by the trappings of friends and relations who would be a bad influence on me.

Today, many parents who have taught their children the ways of God wonder why the same children have lost it.

They become harsh on themselves and end up frustrated and depressed. It is not easy. But what is important is to be content with what they have done for their children. If they have pointed them to Christ and helped them know the way, that ought to be enough. Children, once they have grown, are to make their own decisions. We cannot decide for them. All we know is that, because we have provided correct information on life, they can make an informed decision. We let go and continue praying that they make the right decision. It is tough, but it has to be done.

The billions that inhabit the earth fail every day. They fall short. And God is aware of and understands failure. He doesn't condone stepping over the mark, but he responds well to those who own up and seek to start afresh. He has done so from the very beginning. Many heroes of the faith in history stumbled and fell along the way, but they rose again. They learned the lessons and moved on with greater determination to succeed and make a difference. You are not alone. There is a cloud of witnesses who have gone before you who are cheering you on to stand up and continue walking. To reach your goal. To refuse to be distracted by your failure and to realise that when you come to your senses and acknowledge your failure, you can move forward. You can be put together again by the Creator of the universe. And there are many who are willing to be part of your restoration process. Go on then. Reclaim your original position, and live on.

We are all prodigal sons at one point or the other in our lives. When we fail to live up to what God wants, we have in essence left home and are doing our own thing. When we don't live up to the standards that God has set, we are in a strange land away from our Father. When we don't love others as God loves us, we are lost in our world of hate and need to come back home. Yet each time we wander away from "home," God waits patiently for us to come back. To enjoy the life that he has destined for us from the beginning of the world. He wants to restore us to our original position and help us participate in changing our world and that of others.

Sadly, when we are finally restored, don't expect fanfare and blazing ululation from everyone. Some will sneer at you, while some will be critical of the process of your restoration. Like the brother in the story of the Prodigal Son, they will even complain to God as to why you have been let off the hook when you were supposed to pay the price. They will cry, "Unfair! Unfair!" The older brother became angry and refused to go in. So his father went out and pleaded with him. But he answered his father, "Look! All these years I've been slaving for you and never disobeyed your orders. Yet you never gave me even a young goat so I could celebrate with my friends. But when this son of yours who has squandered your property with prostitutes comes home, you kill the fattened calf for him!" (Luke 15:28–30 NIV).

Why celebrate with someone who messed up from the beginning? What is there to celebrate? Such is the response of many who love sticking to the past and do not enjoy today and tomorrow. They become jealous. But don't be disheartened. They don't understand that your Father in heaven loves you as you are. You are restored because you are loved, in spite of what you have done. The elder son and many today don't get it.

Many times, like the elder son, we despise those who come back from the brink. We wish they were still stuck in their sins and failures. Sometimes we pretend to want them to change. And when they change, we can't handle it. We are not prepared. You see, there is jealousy in us. We can't handle freedom and liberation. We cannot appreciate that the nature of our God is such that he can handle what we call "trash" and mould it into something new. David had a similar attitude.

> Truly God is good to Israel,
> to those who are pure in heart.
> But as for me, my feet had almost stumbled,
> my steps had nearly slipped.
> For I was envious of the arrogant
> when I saw the prosperity of the wicked.
> For they have no pangs until death;
> their bodies are fat and sleek.
>
> (Psalm 73:1–4 ESV)

Whatever people say, what matters is that you are restored. And this is God's core business. He does it well.

CHAPTER 10

From Prison to Praise

Not the physical building. It doesn't have to be. We are all at one time or another prisoners to lust, impatience, and the list goes on. Simon, in the Bible, popular and nicknamed the Great One, was a prisoner of sin. He was entangled in a web he could not come out of. When he saw Peter and John performing miracles, he was envious. He offered them cash. But Peter's diagnosis of Simon's condition was spot on. "For I see that you are in the gall of bitterness and in the bond of iniquity" (Acts 8:23 ESV).

Unfortunately, we are not told what happened to Simon after that. Being bound or a slave to something implies that we can be loosed at some point. And this is the story of the salvation of mankind from the beginning. We hear of many stories, in the Diaspora, of people who became trapped in a web of sin and intrigue. Unable to deliver themselves. With God's help, this has been possible.

What do you consider to be your prison? I mean your Achilles heel. Your weakest link. Something that has dogged you for ages. Consider the following:

George graduated from university with flying colours, including a PhD to crown it all. Intelligent, good-looking, and a gorgeous wife and kids. It started off as infatuation and ended up as something he could not shake off. His conscience had become seared. He became the great pretender. By the time his wife discovered this at church, it was too late. She was devastated. A nervous wreck. They both needed help. He continued going to church to please others and not out of a genuine love for God. He had all the trappings of religion, but without power. Like Simeon, he believed, was baptised but remained his old self.

Many, like George, are broken leaders within the home. Prisoners unable to escape. Many are crying for help but are unheard because society has "legitimised" immoral behaviour. Their children grow without role models.

But God is interested. He is in the salvage business. He restores; he makes people whole again. He does it for a purpose, so that the recovered will help others who are in the same predicament.

Joseph at seventeen found himself serving time in prison. Unbelievable for someone who had so much going for him. A dreamer, his father's favourite son. Prison is tough; those who have been there will tell you. Joseph survived. He made friends. He exercised his God-given gift of interpreting dreams. He came forward. He did not remain in his cocoon when a call was made to interpret other prisoners' dreams. And two years later, he was in the palace. How did he do that? God did it. He remembered Joseph. He was faithful to Joseph's dream. He remained the head and not the tail. No circumstance could suppress his vision.

Joseph must have had moments when he looked back and praised God. One minute he thought he was done by, and the other, he came out triumphant. And everything he touched was successful. Pharaoh's house was blessed because of Joseph. His influence was overwhelming. He was a leader catapulted to greater things by God. He went into prison, might be distraught and sad, but came out leaping and praising God.

It is a fact of life that you will always encounter problems. Such is the predictability of our universe. But thank God that we have the capacity to turn around what seems to be insurmountable challenges. Our prison can be turned into praise.

Paul and Silas in the Bible were accused of "turning the world upside down." They were locked up in the dungeon. It must have been frustrating being locked up for something they had not done.

The kind of prisons Paul and Silas were put into was not comfortable. The authorities made sure that any prisoner's experience was tough and sometimes degrading and dehumanising. They were locked up, and sometimes their legs were tied with iron chains. The inside of the prison looked like a neglected dungeon: cold, dreary, and sometimes damp. Their food was lowered through an opening the size of a manhole.

The guards were usually Roman soldiers. They were under strict orders to guard the prisoners. If any of the prisoners escaped, the guards would be executed. You can imagine what it felt like to be dumped into such a hostile environment. This is why it is striking that Paul and Silas, in such conditions, prayed and sang. It was strange that the prisoners who were supposed to be broken in spirit had the courage and the faith to sing along. Surely they must have had great faith in the God they worshipped. This is a great lesson for many who find themselves giving up because of the situation they find themselves in.

> About midnight Paul and Silas were praying and singing hymns to God, and the prisoners were listening to them.
>
> (Acts 13:25 ESV)

You may not be in a physical prison but in prison. Your challenges may seem insurmountable, but they are surmountable. Your God may be near yet so far, but he is ever present. Take a cue from men and women who have been there, in the dungeon, but came out. Sometimes battered and bruised; rejected but not forsaken. It is not easy, for some have lost their lives in the process, some have been crippled for life, but the pilot light remains deep down in their hearts. Something keeps them going on the journey. They refuse to lose focus. They stick to their goals.

There are many prisons within us. Many of us are caught up in binding thoughts that leave you deflated and unable to go on with your life. Relationships that are manipulative, threatening, and leaving you vulnerable. You may have been there for decades, suffering from a spirit of unforgiveness that is eating you like gangrene. Grossly bloated and stuck in a rut, xenophobic and living a cabbage existence. Surely a prison of all sorts. Thank God, you can break the cycle. You can break the curse. You can be freed. Just like the many people Jesus came into contact with. Some were stuck for years but heeded his call to rise up and walk. And they all did. You can break the glass ceiling. You can walk out through the iron curtain because it is not. It is what Satan says it is. You can cry, "Free at last! Free at last!" What a feeling! But one step at a time.

Expose the prison. Determine to come out of it and make the first step towards the door. Someone may lead you out like Peter who was led out of the prison by an angel. And the church was praying for Peter when this happened. Have others who will be standing in the gap for you. This is crucial. You are not an island. They will celebrate your release with you. They will beat the drums of joy. This is certain. Thanks be to God who gives us victory through our Lord Jesus Christ. "So if the Son sets you free, you will be free indeed" (John 8:36). And this is certain because of what God has done to so many.

We are all at risk. We all need to be vigilant, all the time. When darkness comes over us, we need to realise who is there to enable us to remove the *shackles that entangle us.*

Some sat in darkness, in utter darkness,
prisoners suffering in iron chains,
because they rebelled against God's commands
and despised the plans of the Most High.
So he subjected them to bitter labor;
they stumbled, and there was no one to help.
Then they cried to the Lord in their trouble,
and he saved them from their distress.
He brought them out of darkness, the utter darkness,
and broke away their chains.
Let them give thanks to the Lord for his unfailing love
and his wonderful deeds for mankind,
for he breaks down gates of bronze
and cuts through bars of iron.

(Psalm 107:10 NIV)

The reality is that we cannot do it on our own. It is important for us to be part of the solution, as we believe that it can happen. But we have a God who is skilled in rescue operations. For those in situations that are tough and difficult. As the old hymn says,

What a Friend we have in Jesus,
All our sins and griefs to bear!
What a privilege to carry
Everything to God in prayer!
O what peace we often forfeit,
O what needless pain we bear,

All because we do not carry
Everything to God in prayer!

Have we trials and temptations?
Is there trouble anywhere?
We should never be discouraged,
Take it to the Lord in prayer.
Can we find a friend so faithful
Who will all our sorrows share?
Jesus knows our every weakness,
Take it to the Lord in prayer.

Are we weak and heavy-laden,
Cumbered with a load of care?
Precious Savior, still our refuge—
Take it to the Lord in prayer;
Do thy friends despise, forsake thee?
Take it to the Lord in prayer;
In His arms He'll take and shield thee,
Thou wilt find a solace there.
(Joseph M. Scriven)

No matter how tough it is, there is always a way out. However deep and dreary the prison is, there is always a way. That is the great potential that Jesus has put in us. The ability to wriggle out of despair and into the wonderful opportunities that God has in store for us. He opens our eyes to see the opportunities yonder. To realise that where we are is not where will be tomorrow. Our setbacks are only for a season. Opportunity keeps knocking on the door, if only we could realise that. And this is what every one of us faces all the time. Times of setbacks meant to provide lessons for us. This is the stuff that we are all made of, and we should expect this all the time.

Many of us are caged in, unable to wriggle out of our prisons. These include depression, feelings of guilt, anxiety, childhood memories, and exploitation. We cry every day for someone to rescue us, but our voices do not get far enough. A wife daily battered by an abusive husband. A child on the verge of committing suicide because he is trapped in his own home. A child bullied at school or on the Internet. All these are prisons of sorts.

This is where help is needed, to come out of such predicaments. While some can find the will to come out on their own, for many, there is need for outside intervention. This is how we can turn prison into praise.

CHAPTER 11

Beyond Pain

The world today is being defined by tragedy. The carnage, be it on the roads, the sea, or in the air. Massacres of innocent citizens across the globe flood the news daily. We are at a tipping point. And in all this is a mother, a father, a son, and a daughter grieving for their loved ones. For them it's beyond pain as Sir Bob Geldof summed it up after his daughter died tragically in England.

How do you console individuals who have lost their loved ones in such tragic circumstances? Or a relation who has succumbed to cancer? The pain, the hurt, the loss is unbearable. We try. Others have tried when we are faced with the same predicament. But boy, isn't it difficult? Where do you start? Many have not recovered. And some have taken their lives as they could not handle it. Their emotions just gave in. Sad.

But some have turned beauty for ashes. Their brokenness as a result has been reconstituted into something worthwhile. They have stood up again, and they have renewed their faith in the God who cares. But it has been a process. A long and winding road, a journey. You might be on that journey still. It still hurts. You are still beyond pain. Hold on.

Job in the Bible went through a similar experience. Unfortunately his wife was not helpful. "Curse God and die." His friends too found it difficult to comfort him, as they rationalised the whole tragedy, arguing that he may have displeased God. But throughout Job's argument with his friends is the acknowledgement of the sovereignty of God. That he is in control, he is still on the throne. He was convinced that what mattered to him was that he was going to see God in the end. That God would vindicate him. That suffering was an unpalatable package in the scheme of things. Painful, but God always sees us through the tragedies of life. We may not have the answers, but that does not lessen the grace and power of God, and his love never fails in spite of what we go through. And bad things happen to good people all the time.

If you are distraught because of a bereavement, you are not alone. Nor will you walk alone. The key is to accept that it is not easy. There are no quick fixes. Those who have overcome tragedy do so in pain and hurt. They are bruised and battered. But like Paul in the Bible, they have a faith that they will come through.

> We are hard pressed on every side, but not crushed; perplexed, but not in despair; persecuted, but not abandoned; struck down, but not destroyed. We always carry around in our body the death of Jesus, so that the life of Jesus may also be revealed in our body.
>
> (2 Corinthians 4:8 NIV)

How this works in practice depends on how you clutch on to the promises of God. Share with others who have gone through similar experiences. Pray, seek counsel, and just have a dogged determination to overcome. Your piece, a difficult one, can be picked by God. He cares. He has promised to care. "Cast all your anxiety on him because he cares for you" (1 Peter 5:7 NIV). Notice it's casting, throwing, getting rid of our anxieties. A tough assignment.

It is when it hurts so bad that we need to look to turn to someone able to deal with our hurt and pain.

It is when we acknowledge our pain, share it, and seek help in the company of those whose hearts bleed for us that we experience relief. Just to know someone cares does make a difference.

You may think you blew it in childhood or as a teenager. That the baggage is too much. But again, you are not alone. Leave it and cleave to the new you, to the future. God is in the salvage business, and you're his target. Wow!

How do you deal with pain when it is unbearable? When your hope in people is suddenly taken away from you, how do you cope? When the mother who was your backbone in life is suddenly dying of cancer, how do you handle it? And when she is taken away from you in pain, emaciated by the disease, who is there to help?

Not so long ago, a friend succumbed to a triple form of cancer. She was strong and reassuring each time we spoke to her. When we attended her son's wedding, she travelled thousands of miles from Zimbabwe. At the wedding, she appeared strong. She was blessed with an infectious smile that came from her deep belief in a God who cares. A God who cares beyond pain. She was the star at her son's wedding and enjoyed it to the full. Not long after this, she was in great pain, and slowly her health deteriorated. Yet among those who cared for her, including doctors and nurses, they were struck by her resilience and her smile and positivity in the midst of such a debilitating disease. One of the doctors even asked to be prayed for by her. What a testimony. A year later, when she passed away, I was asked to conduct her funeral in Orange County in the USA. What an experience it was. The realisation that, even when it hurts so bad and it is beyond pain, greater goodness can come out of it. I was emotional, and so were her husband, son, and daughter. Friends and relations were devastated, but her smile was the backdrop even when this tragedy struck. This piece comes from the way I was inspired by her having known her and her husband for more than forty years. I was the best man at their wedding then, and here I was saying farewell to her at her funeral. I was inspired to write this poem, which I read at the funeral:

Behind That Smile
Behind that smile was a faith so strong.
A dogged determination to succeed, to endure.
Behind that smile was a caring heart.
Behind that smile was a stubborn resistance against disease,
A love that embraced all.

Behind that smile was a mother's love,

A love that went beyond pain.

Behind that smile was a courage that knew no boundaries,

A love so strong you could not say goodbye.

Job experienced pain at its best. The loss of everything that he counted *worthy*: his children, animals, fields. All that defined the rich and famous of his time. And then his body crumbled and daily he was in pain.

How do you comfort such a person? How do you console them? Yet God had a way for him. He gave him the strength to carry on. He had a faith in a God who was in the business of picking up the pieces.

I know that my redeemer lives,

and that in the end he will stand on the earth.

And after my skin has been destroyed,

yet in my flesh I will see God;

I myself will see him

with my own eyes—I, and not another.

How my heart yearns within me!

(Job 19:25–29 NIV)

Job saw beyond pain. He believed in a God who would take him beyond his present circumstances. Beyond sickness, loss, hurt, and pain into what God intends for us. Allow us to see the end from the beginning. To focus not on yesterday but tomorrow. Paul says,

> That is why I am suffering as I am. Yet this is no cause for shame, because I know whom I have believed, and am convinced that he is able to guard what I have entrusted to him until that day.
>
> (2 Timothy 1:12)

Paul knew why he was suffering. He did not see it as the end but the beginning. A confirmation of whom he believed in. A demonstration to everyone in doubt that he was not alone but was rooted and grounded in the person of Jesus Christ. He would sustain, strengthen, and protect Paul, and he would see him at the end.

We will suffer pain at one point in our lives. This is inevitable. Through losing a loved one, going through suffering as a result of a terminal illness like cancer, or a victim of a horrific accident that lives us crippled for life. Our friends and relations may be going through any of the categories mentioned. Whichever form it takes and however it happens, pain is pain. The challenge is how to manage it. How do you go through life in such circumstances? There are no schools that prepare you for this. You have to deal with it yourself when it comes. Sometimes, and in most cases, we are ill prepared for it. Other times, we are prepared for it theoretically yet lack the experience to physically go through it in real life.

I have gone through pain and loss. While friends have sometimes made a difference, I have found that the thing that helps set the healing process in motion is acknowledging that it has happened. That this is now the situation and, as my wife puts it, it is the "new normal." I will have to live with it for now, and maybe longer, until it eventually disappears in my mental archives. Here it will lie dormant and incapable of reactivating my source of pain and sorrow. Here is emotional education that is not taught in any school, but only the school of life. Your pain will not go away, but it will be managed so that you are in the driving seat and can dictate how it will affect you. You are in control. Not your friends. Not your doctor.

We hear of people with mental illnesses who are great painters. They use their skill to manage their situation. It does not take away the condition, but it makes them take the reins and use their skill for their own good and for the good of the community. Wow!

Accept the "new normal" and try not to fight it. If it is the loss of a loved won, acknowledge what has happened and always remind yourself that life has to go on. This is a basic law. Something happens that may interrupt the rhythm of life, but the heart of life beats on. Things don't fall apart, but they may be rearranged as an oddity. Period. Truth is too naked. That is why it does not excite man. Once you master this, you are on the road to becoming a consultant. One who shall in the future help others who will travel on the same road you are travelling now. So there is an upside to every downside of life. So keep holding on, and keep learning from the new normal.

When there seems to be no let-up in your pain and distress and it is consistent, seek help. Many people have soldiered on and sought to become heroes when inside they are hurting. It is not necessary. It's amazing how much professional counsel exists. And if such a resource is exploited early, many issues may be resolved and lives saved. One of the reasons broken people take their own lives is that they cannot be courageous enough to seek help. Counsel helps you to see things differently.

Adopt an open-door policy. Don't shy away from other people. We were meant to be a community. No man is an island. And there is something that happens when we open up to others and do not isolate ourselves. There is an environment of goodwill that is released and that makes part of our healing process. Suddenly, other experiences are shared and we begin to realise that ours is only a speck on the grand scheme of things. That we are the umpteenth person that has suffered loss and moved on; that we are only a speck of dust among the many who have been broken. Suddenly, we converse with others who have been there before and survived. Mere mortal beings less resilient, weaker, and more vulnerable. And all of a sudden, the "I can" mindset plays in your mind. What a relief. It still hurts, you still suffer loss, but you are not alone. You are community. It's far better.

God Values You

God has put a high value on those he has created. You. No ifs or buts. That is how he regards us. And because we are high value, we are exposed to the Enemy. The one who grins at seeing us walk tall proud of who we are before God. The temptation is that we regard ourselves as not valuable. Always. Especially when you have gone through the toughest experience in your life. You have been exposed, run down, and vulnerable. That is when the small voice comes through suggesting that you have had it. You are weak and not strong. You are done. This is the end for you. No one will pick up your pieces.

If there is one thing Jesus did well among the many, he reminded his followers who they were before him. Their importance, their value, and their difference from all else God created. And he brings in the little versatile sparrow as a comparison. A bird that flies thousands of miles in formation over seas, mountains, and rugged terrain but still survives. If God can care for a tiny meatless bird like the sparrow, what about you? You who were created in the image of God. You in whom God breathed his very life. If the sparrow is fearless as it flies across the globe, why not you?

God cares. We may not esteem the tiny sparrow, but Jesus used it to illustrate our heavenly Father's watchful care. "You are of more value than many sparrows" (Matthew 10:31). If God is concerned about the tiny sparrow, how much greater must his concern be for man, who is immeasurably greater in value than the sparrow?

There is no place for worry in the life of a sparrow, and no attempt to stockpile supplies for the future—yet their lives go on. The point Jesus is making is not that the birds do not work; it has been said that no one works harder than a sparrow to make a living; the point He is making is that they do not worry. Sparrows do not strain to see into a future, which they cannot see, and do not seek to find security in the things they have accumulated for the future.

(The Church of Christ in Zion, Badfield.com)

He will pick up the pieces of your life. He will make you into what he has designed you to be. He loves you. He cares for you. You are special. Fear not, for he is with you.

> You whom I took from the ends of the earth,
> and called from its farthest corners,
> saying to you, "You are my servant,
> I have chosen you and not cast you off";
> fear not, for I am with you;
> be not dismayed, for I am your God;
> I will strengthen you, I will help you,
> I will uphold you with my righteous right hand.
>
> (Isaiah 41:9–10 ESV)

No wonder you are a target. You should not be surprised when the going gets tough and you find yourself under siege from everywhere. You are high value. You have special protection. And someone is out to get you. All the time. Tough!

God adds value to mankind. He pronounced it from the beginning when he made man and woman in his own image. Man was in a sorry state. He was doomed. But God transformed man and gave him new life. He breathed his Spirit in man and new life was born. Thus he added value. That is why we are more valuable than many sparrows. He did not make us different but like him. This is the greatest honour that God can give. "Yet you have made him a little lower than the heavenly beings and crowned him with glory and honor" (Psalm 8:5 ESV).

This is how God looks at us. This is why he is a jealous God. Preserving and protecting his creation.

Man was made from dust, ordinary dust, but his value was added when God breathed the Holy Spirit in him. He was made in charge of the earth and given the responsibility of taking care of it. That is who you are. You are unique. You are special. You have power. God has added value on your life and well-being.

This is why he is always on the lookout for you, to salvage you. To restore you. To protect you. Because you are worthy, valuable. This is why on Easter Friday we remember the final act of Jesus: dying for mankind. Dealing with the problem of sin once and for all.

When you cry unto the Lord, things happen.

To God, no job is too big or too small. Once you connect with him, he responds. He needs no prompting. You tell him, and he listens. He remembers and does not forget. David in the Bible wrote a psalm which clearly demonstrates the nature of

God and his attitude towards those who mess up but still cry to him.

> Oh, give thanks to the Lord, for He is good! For His mercy endures forever. Let the redeemed of the Lord say so, Whom He has redeemed from the hand of the enemy, And gathered out of the lands, From the east and from the west, From the north and from the south. They wandered in the wilderness in a desolate way; They found no city to dwell in. Hungry and thirsty, Their soul fainted in them. Then they cried out to the Lord in their trouble, And He delivered them out of their distresses. And He led them forth by the right way, That they might go to a city for a dwelling place. Oh, that men would give thanks to the Lord for His goodness, And for His wonderful works to the children of men! For He satisfies the longing soul, And fills the hungry soul with goodness. Those who sat in darkness and in the shadow of death, Bound in affliction and irons—Because they rebelled against the words of God, And despised the counsel of the Most High, Therefore He brought down their heart with labour; They fell down, and there was none to help. Then they cried out to the Lord in their trouble, And He saved them out of their distresses. He brought them out of darkness and the shadow of death, And broke their chains in pieces. Oh, that men would give thanks to the Lord for His goodness, And for His wonderful works to the children

of men! For He has broken the gates of bronze, And cut the bars of iron in two. Fools, because of their transgression, And because of their iniquities, were afflicted. Their soul abhorred all manner of food, And they drew near to the gates of death. Then they cried out to the Lord in their trouble, And He saved them out of their distresses. He sent His word and healed them, And delivered them from their destructions. Oh, that men would give thanks to the Lord for His goodness, And for His wonderful works to the children of men! Let them sacrifice the sacrifices of thanksgiving, And declare His works with rejoicing. Those who go down to the sea in ships, Who do business on great waters, They see the works of the Lord, And His wonders in the deep. For He commands and raises the stormy wind, Which lifts up the waves of the sea. They mount up to the heavens, They go down again to the depths; Their soul melts because of trouble. They reel to and fro, and stagger like a drunken man, And are at their wit's end. Then they cry out to the Lord in their trouble, And He brings them out of their distresses. He calms the storm, So that its waves are still. Then they are glad because they are quiet; So He guides them to their desired haven. Oh, that men would give thanks to the Lord for His goodness, And for His wonderful works to the children of men! Let them exalt Him also in the assembly of the people, And praise Him in the company of the elders. He turns rivers into a wilderness, And the water springs into dry ground; A fruitful land into barrenness, For the wickedness of those who dwell in it. He turns a wilderness into pools of water, And dry land into water springs. There He makes the hungry dwell, That they may establish a city for a dwelling place, And sow fields and plant vineyards, That they may yield a fruitful harvest. He also blesses them, and they multiply greatly; And He does not let their cattle decrease. When they are diminished and brought low Through oppression, affliction and sorrow, He pours contempt on princes, And causes them to wander in the wilderness where there is no way; Yet He sets the poor on high, far from affliction, And makes their families like a flock. The righteous see it and rejoice, And all iniquity stops its mouth. Whoever is wise will observe these things, And they will understand the lovingkindness of the Lord.

(Psalm 107 NIV)

This is a psalm of hope. However broken you are. Whatever situation has let you down. Whatever circumstances that seem unbearable and beyond salvaging, God provides the answer. He is there. He hears. He is ready to intervene. Always. It matters not how you are bound. It matters not how you have messed up. His loving-kindness is above any hurt and pain. What a God. In a world where you can be forgotten, thrown into the dustbin of history. You may be despised, forsaken, and stigmatised, yet there is hope in God. What a relief!

The people identified in the psalm of David had abandoned God, they were wandering in the desert, and they had made fools of themselves. Despite all this, God comes through as a merciful God. He turns tragic situations into blessings. All he expects of you is that you share with him, cry to him, and acknowledge your predicament.

This is the tragedy. This is what many people go through every day. They have given up. They think their situations are impossible. No one can help. But we have a God whose core business is looking for those who have given up and raising their hopes. Finding the lost and restoring them to their original positions. The errant son who has not communicated with his parents for twenty years, the husband who loathes his wife, and the wife who is on the verge of going out with another man. God says, "Come unto me, you who are heavy laden, and I will give you rest." Rest? Yes, relaxation and comfort. Contentment knowing that someone has taken charge of the challenges you face. His invitation is non-discriminatory. It doesn't matter what you have gone through or what you have done. It is an open invitation. It doesn't matter when you did it to whom and how serious the matter is. Still come. A convicted robber, a murderer, a lady of the night, a womaniser. Still come. "Come, let us reason together, says the Lord, though your sins are as scarlet, they shall be as white as snow."

You may be harbouring feelings of hate and unforgiveness. You may have done something you have not quite talked about and it's eating you inside. Whatever it is, come. Take it to the Lord in prayer. Share it with a confidant. Experience freedom when you do it, because God understands we are feeble and are but dust. He doesn't treat us the way he ought to because of that.

> Just as a father has compassion on *his* children,
> So the LORD has compassion on those who fear Him.
> For He Himself knows our frame;
> He is mindful that we are *but* dust
>
> (Psalm 103:13–15 NASB)

What a difference God is to men and women we interact with on a daily basis: judgemental, condescending, and dismissive. You do one thing wrong and you are condemned outright. Your record remains intact. Reference is made to it each time you do something wrong. It's indirect blackmail. You are a prisoner. Not with God. Not when you cry to him. It is finished. Jesus cried on the cross. He dealt with the effect of sin once and for all. Thank God. We are free indeed!

Because God is a Creator, he has deposited the creative potential in all of us. So God can turn rivers into deserts and deserts into rivers. This means he can turn impossible situations into potentially great and positive ones. He can turn a down-and-out into a skilled artisan, a painter who can impact the world. The following case studies illustrate this.

As a young man, Abraham Lincoln went to war a captain and returned a private. Afterwards, he was a failure as a businessman. As a lawyer in Springfield, he was too impractical and temperamental to be a success. He turned to politics and was defeated in his first try for the legislature. He was again defeated in his first attempt to be nominated for Congress, defeated in his application to be commissioner of the General Land Office, defeated in the senatorial election of 1854, defeated in his efforts for the vice presidency in 1856, and defeated in the senatorial election of 1858. At about that time, he wrote in a letter to a friend, "I am now the most miserable man living. If what I feel were equally distributed to the whole human family, there would not be one cheerful face on the earth."

Winston Churchill repeated a grade during elementary school, and when he entered Harrow, he was placed in the lowest division of the lowest class. Later, he twice failed the entrance exam to the Royal Military Academy at Sandhurst. He was defeated in his first effort to serve in Parliament. He became prime minister at the age of sixty-two. He later wrote, "Never give in, never give in, never, never, never, never—in nothing, great or small, large or petty—never give in except to convictions of honour and good sense. Never, Never, Never, Never give up." *His* capitals, mind you.

The above stories are proof of how situations can suddenly change for a person. Once a nobody but later a somebody whose influence amazes the world. There is still hope for the hopeless, courage for the discouraged, and motivation for the demotivated. Are you at the end of your tether? Do you feel it's the last straw? Take courage. Never, never, never, give up. Abraham Lincoln didn't, and Winston Churchill didn't either. And the heroes in the Bible—Joseph, Deborah, and Paul—didn't.

Many people are still broken. For some, this has been a lifelong experience. Unending, it seems. Is there a way out or is this the end? We all have the capacity to wriggle out of the impossible. No one is created to be doomed. That is the message of this book and many other books that have been written on this subject. You cannot wallow in your failure. You should not give up because others gave up. Keep trying, and with God on your side, it will happen in your own way, in your own time. Stories of other men and women who made it should be an encouragement.

CHAPTER 12

When Life Pales into Insignificance

The normal expression is "pale into insignificance." To pale is to fade away. To pale into insignificance is to fade away to virtually nothing. If something pales into insignificance, it does not seem at all important when compared to something else. When your child's ill, everything else pales into insignificance. With the outbreak of war, all else fades into insignificance. But *pale in significance* is also heard, which means something is *less* important than before.

When you are broken and the pieces don't seem to come together, life seems meaningless. This is when you analyse the situation. This is when things that seem to matter pale into insignificance when compared to the new reality. If need be, you need to reposition yourself to face the new reality. Strategize, plan, and reprogramme your life. At last you realise what life really means. The core, the centre of it, and not the periphery.

It is when you are told you have a few days or months to live that you want to make up with those whom you haven't been in good books for years. It is when your loving ones die that you wish you had had quality time with them. The holiday you meant to have but didn't happen in the end. The visits, the fellowship, and the get-togethers that never happened. Then you realise that life is more than the things that you valued in your life. That there is so much that you could have done that you didn't do. Suddenly, the weightier matters of life that Jesus mentioned to the Pharisees come to the fore.

> Woe to you, scribes and Pharisees, hypocrites! For you tithe mint and dill and cumin, and have neglected the weightier matters of the law: justice and mercy and faithfulness. These you ought to have done, without neglecting the others.
>
> (Matthew 23:23 ESV)

How often we neglect important matters in life. And when we are broken, that is when we realise that there are more important things than our present predicament. It is tough, yes. But this cannot erode the very essence of life. Life holds in the midst of great storms, tsunamis, and the lot. What God has destined in our lives is not swept away because we have been broken and our lives are in tatters.

When one close to us suffers from Alzheimer's and can hardly do the things they used to. A great speaker, engineer, or nurse turned to confusion and unable to remember things. What matters now is that they are there with them. That they are able to do vital things that enable them to live a fulfilled life even in their present condition. Ability to walk, to eat, to smile, to sleep, and to laugh when they can. How valuable these things are. Small daily miracles that keep the family going. That becomes life. It is the stuff that makes everyone joyful and look forward to seeing every day. I remember a great brother and friend who, when I met him several years ago, could not recognise who I was. He now suffers from dementia. He had been a gifted speaker of international fame but was confined to his house. His wife was looking after him. And for him, it is the little matters of life that matter. A laugh, a smile. Small daily miracles that keep the family going. That now have become the life. It is the stuff that makes everyone joyful and look forward to seeing a new day.

You see, when you are broken and everything else around you is disintegrating, there are still nuggets of gold spread out in your life. Things that you can look forward to—small mercies to be grateful for. God's light still shines in the midst of confusion and despondency. God's light shines through the circumstances and situations that seem insurmountable. Your focus is on the things that are value added and what you considered to be the things that matter. You prioritise. You set the agenda. You set goals—realistic goals. And your attitude to those around you is transformed. You value every minute you spend with them. You are more than just a body. You are more valuable than many sparrows. You are God's child, and you appreciate it.

What is significant becomes that which will last a lifetime. Relationships, love, joy, and peace. The things that enhance your life and which remain constant. As Jesus said,

Then he said to them, "Watch out! Be on your guard against all kinds of greed; life does not consist in an abundance of possessions."

(Luke 12:15)

He goes on to tell a parable of the rich fool who had everything but little regard for the things that matter. His life was taken away as he was on the verge of expanding his kingdom to serve his personal interests. Jesus was teaching that there is much more to life than possessions. You need to find that which makes life worthwhile in order to live beyond the brokenness and the pain of this world.

It's easy to assume that life would be a breeze if we had unlimited wealth, but money truly can't buy happiness. Many times you read or hear stories of young men and women who had it so good in life but who secretly suffered emotional and physical hardships, addictions, and abuse that made their lives miserable.

Many people are broken even when they seemingly have it all. They have insatiable appetites for those habits that kill and do not enhance life. They go for the jugular when it comes to sex, money, and drugs. It is when they come to their senses that the real work begins as society tries hard to rehabilitate them and restore them to their former self. It is hard work. A colleague of mine has struggled with her son who has been in and out of rehabilitation centres. Each time he is on the verge of drying out, he relapses and falls back to the bottle. Then they start all over again. His mother has lost hope and has decided not to entertain him whenever he comes home while high on the elements. Her son's brokenness has led to her brokenness too. And this is repeated in many households across the world. And this where the pieces of people's lives have to be picked up. It is tough. It is a process and God's core business. As we acknowledge the reality of what is happening, it is important to seek help as well as to have hope and faith in a God who cares.

There is a story in the Bible of Jesus's encounter with a man who lived in tombs. This man was so strong that even when they tied him with chains, he would break them. He was uncontrollable. No one could stop him until Jesus showed up. The story concludes as follows: "When they came to Jesus, they saw the man who had been possessed by the legion of demons, sitting there, dressed and in his right mind; and they were afraid." (Mark 5:15 NIV).

How did Jesus do it? Whatever led this man to doing what he did was not as powerful as Jesus. The man's power was no match for the Creator of the universe. When God intervened, things changed and the community around took notice. This has not changed even today. When we are broken, we can expect God to be there when we need him and make things happen.

We cannot run away from trouble and misfortune but we can survive when we realise the importance of depending on God. Realisation that what we have comes from him and we are merely stewards given the responsibility to administer it responsibly.

Our preoccupation should be to reflect on those values that will sustain us through thick and thin. As Paul says,

> Finally, brothers, whatever is true, whatever is honourable, whatever is just, whatever is pure, whatever is lovely, whatever is commendable, if there is any excellence, if there is anything worthy of praise, think about these things.
>
> (Philippians 4:8 ESV)

Such a mindset changes the dynamic of our life. It energises us and helps us focus on the true essence of life. It crowds out the chaff in our lives and attracts noble thoughts to relive again in us. It separates the dross from pure silver and presents the finished product of life for others to see and emulate. Welcome to life as God intended it!

You now focus on issues and not tissues. You remain unmoved, rooted, and grounded in the love of God. You pick and choose your agenda, and you are not distracted by what others throw at you—even "holy gossip"! You are your own person who is ready to accomplish your destiny, even in the valley of the shadow of death. When all else seems to be going against you, remain resolute and concentrate on the weightier matters of life. This is an endangered species in our world. A people who are looking unto Jesus, always. A people anxious to do the will of God and not their will. A people enduring until the end in the midst of a world that is giving up as it struggles to be politically correct. In a dog-eat-dog world, the church of Jesus Christ remains true to its call. To do the will of him who sent it. To follow in his footsteps. You are a member of this great body of Christ. And together as members under the headship of Christ, nothing will separate us from the love of God in Christ Jesus.

This is the greatest challenge we face today. The propagation of the message of Jesus Christ and its saving and loving power. The immutability of a God who through prayer can change circumstances and situations. A God who can heal and restore that which has been stolen from you. A truthful and faithful God. When you stake your position unashamedly and live a life that exposes those values, strongholds will be moved. And you will never be the same again and even those you interact with will be affected if not infected!

It is true that things that matter can pale into insignificance. When my daughter, who had just completed her law degree, was diagnosed with an illness, she admitted, "Dad, my hopes for the future and the things that mattered to me most have now paled into significance as I realise that my life is now at stake." How true. She realise that a career as a solicitor, though important, could not match the new priorities in her life, now that she was uncertain about her future. And for us her family, just having her was more important than what we hoped she would be in the future. Suddenly we valued her more now than tomorrow. We wanted to love her now than yesterday.

What are your priorities? What things matter to you, and how do they match up to life as God intended it to be? You may need to reorder these priorities so you keep focused on God's purpose for you in this life. Paul said,

> I don't know what will happen to me in Jerusalem, but I must obey God's Spirit and go there. In every city I visit, I am told by the Holy Spirit that I will be put in jail and will be in trouble in Jerusalem. But I don't care what happens to me, as long as I finish the work that the Lord Jesus gave me to do. And that work is to tell the good news about God's great kindness.
>
> (Acts 20:22–24 CEV)

Thankfully, Paul did accomplish his mission. He fought the good fight, he finished the race, and he kept the faith. Nothing deterred him from his mission. Will you do that too? Now?

We all take things for granted: life, time, friends, work, health, etc. Each new day becomes ordinary as we fail to appreciate the value of being. Until something happens. An illness, a tragedy, a loss. Then blink; it registers. What really matters comes to the fore. That appreciation catapults us to another level. We see beyond our immediate predicament. We push ourselves further towards our goal. We forget about the state we are in and reach out to the One who can get us out of the quagmire and into the starry light that transforms broken pieces into gems of life.

I have come across individuals with multiple sclerosis. This is a depressing disease that slowly affects your whole body. And over time, you are unable to do much. While you expect many to give up, it is surprising that the stronger ones will do as much as they can while it is possible. This means doing as much as they can for as long as they can. This "I can" attitude has helped many to live with their condition productively. During the London or New York marathons, many people do sponsored runs in support of people with MS. This always gives those in this predicament a boost and keeps their hopes alive, even when they know that it is only a matter of time. Their quality of life is enhanced and they try to live life to the max. Well done. What a challenge.

We will not be spared such difficult times in our lives, but these stories illustrate the possibilities there are. That it is never the end, whatever your diagnosis, your circumstance, or your predicament. It is imperative that you move on. And the story of King David, after he had committed not only adultery but also murder of the husband of the woman he had had sex with, is touching.

How did he pick up the pieces of a broken life? Chapter 12 of 2 Samuel gives us some success principles from the life of David in overcoming family failures. Do what David did to pick up the pieces of your broken life. He put priority on worship.

> Then David arose from the earth and washed and anointed himself and changed his clothes. And he went into the house of the LORD and worshiped. He then went to his own house. And when he asked, they set food before him, and he ate. Then his servants said to

him, "What is this thing that you have done? You fasted and wept for the child while he was alive; but when the child died, you arose and ate food." He said, "While the child was still alive, I fasted and wept, for I said, 'Who knows whether the LORD will be gracious to me, that the child may live?' But now he is dead. Why should I fast? Can I bring him back again? I shall go to him, but he will not return to me."

(2 Samuel 12:20–23 ESV)

This was the beginning of David's restoration. He deliberately decided not to remain where he was before. Yes, he acknowledged the wrong he had done, the sin he had committed, but he decided to move on.

You may be a single mother and wonder, after all that has happened to you, how you can pick up the pieces. How you can cope with the rigours of being single and having a family to take care of. God is still in the business of picking up the pieces of single mothers or fathers.

Many single mothers have hit rock bottom. They have seen it all: beatings, abuse, and isolation from a world that preaches inclusiveness. They have been discriminated against. Trying to make ends meet, they wake up early, get the kids to school, and then dash to the office, care home, hospital, or factory. Same routine day in day out. Tired, stressed, and exhausted. No one to cry to. Get to church, and sometimes sense people are not welcoming enough. Dash back home. Struggle to have time to pray and read the Bible.

Many give up and end up either succumbing to alcohol or in other cases taking one's life. The pressure is on. Definitely there is task overload. They cannot manage and still lead a normal life. They are on the edge all the time and need help at the appropriate time. The children suffer as they don't get the attention they deserve. But like the widow, the orphan, and the single mother, God is still in the business of picking up the pieces. The single mother is unique. It is not the past but the present and the future that now matter with God. It is help for today and not what happened yesterday that matters. Once God deals with the past, he deals with it once and for all. And the single mother can come to God with her head raised high and she will receive God's love in time of her need. Day in and day out.

It is not easy for one still fighting her divorce and experiencing abuse in the process. It is not easy when the in-laws are not being helpful. But one's self-esteem can still be restored. One can find solace in the fact that while many have gone through such times, equally many have found their way back, bruised but not broken.

But we still believe that God is in the business of picking up the pieces. How he does it, it's hard to know. But he does it. He has done it to hundreds of single mothers who are now content and satisfied of their lot. Still difficult to steer the terrain, but possible.

Faith has inspired single mothers to meet the challenges head on. In the Bible, we read of a gallant woman, Annah, who was married for only seven years and became a single mother at age eighty-four. Her secret: fasting and praying in the temple every day. A commitment and dedication to God that never wavered. That is why she is remembered.

> There was also a prophet, Anna, the daughter of Penuel, of the tribe of Asher. She was very old; she had lived with her husband seven years after her marriage, and then was a widow until she was eighty-four. She never left the temple but worshiped night and day, fasting and praying.
>
> (Luke 2:36–38 NIV)

She is not the only one. Dorcas, an astute businesswoman, championed the cause of Christ. She challenged Paul to start a church by the riverside in Philippi when she was converted to Christianity. She led a congregation by the riverside.

You have to find your way of dealing with the challenges. God is always at the ready to help in times of trouble. Women of faith preserve. They create. They initiate. Dorcas started a movement of the gospel singlehandedly, with God on her side. You may be a single mum, abandoned and with no one to turn to, but you can rise up again. You can show what you are made of. That you are unique; that you can do it. God is on your side. The King of Kings is at the ready to give you help. When the time has fully come, God will reveal his plan for you. A plan to sustain you, to give you hope in a hopeless environment. Keep looking, keep believing, and keep hoping. It is well with your soul.

The lyrics from this famous song sum it up.

> When peace, like a river, attendeth my way,
> When sorrows like sea billows roll;
> Whatever my lot, Thou hast taught me to say,
> It is well, it is well with my soul.
>> Refrain:
>> It is well with my soul,
>> It is well, it is well with my soul.
> Though Satan should buffet, though trials should come,
> Let this blest assurance control,
> That Christ hath regarded my helpless estate,
> And hath shed His own blood for my soul.
>> (Horatio G. Spafford)

In the 1870s, Spafford was a very successful lawyer in Chicago and heavily invested in real estate. In 1871, the great Chicago fire destroyed all of his downtown investment properties.

In 1873, he and his family planned a vacation trip to Europe. While in Great Britain, he planned to help his good friend, Dwight L. Moody, and Ira Sankey, whom he had financially supported, with their evangelistic tour. Spafford sent his wife and four girls—ages eleven, nine, seven, and two—ahead while he finished up last-minute business in Chicago. On November 22, the S.S. *Ville Du Havre* struck another ship and sank within twelve minutes. Mrs Spafford cabled her husband, "Saved alone."

One story reports that Spafford wrote, "It Is Well with My Soul," while passing over the very spot of the ocean where his four daughters perished, while another, more reliable report, claims he wrote it two years later when Moody and Sankey were visiting his home.

But the tragedy surrounding the hymn didn't end there. Horatio and Anna returned to Chicago and gave birth to Horatio II, who would die at four years old of scarlet fever in 1876. Two years later, the couple gave birth to Bertha, who would write that her parents not only suffered the pain of losing their fortune and five children, but it was compounded by a crisis of faith. Were the children's deaths a punishment from God? Did he no longer love them? Horatio felt himself in danger of losing his faith.

In 1881, Anna gave birth to a sixth daughter, appropriately named Grace. Shortly after, the family of four moved to Jerusalem, with Horatio explaining, "Jerusalem is where my Lord lived, suffered, and conquered, and I wish to learn how to live, suffer, and especially to conquer."

The family would remain in Jerusalem and set up a children's home. And like his children, he too would die tragically. Some reports claim he began to suffer delusions that he was the second Messiah, while his family insists it was the malaria fever from which he died that caused the mental confusion.

But the tragedy surrounding the hymn didn't end there either. The tune was written by Philip P. Bliss, which he entitled "Ville du Havre," the name of the ship that took the lives of Spafford's four daughters. The hymn was first sung by

Bliss himself before a large gathering of ministers hosted by Moody on November 24, 1876.

Just one month later, on December 29, 1876, Bliss and wife were travelling to Chicago by train. As the train passed over a trestle near Ashtabula, Ohio, the bridge collapsed and the passenger coaches plunged seventy-five feet into the icy river. Philip was able to escape through a window, but his wife was pinned in the wreckage. As he went back to free his wife, a fire broke out through the wooden cars and both were burned beyond recognition.

Nine tragic deaths surround the hymn, yet those affected by them could say, "It is well with my soul."

God is in the business of picking up your pieces: bereavement, loss of a loved one, depression, joblessness, just mere lack of motivation, feeling of wanting to quit, suicidal tendencies, self-harm. You matter more than things. You are valuable. You are unique. You are a force to be reckoned with. You can make a difference where you are. Let God release the potential in you. Stand up and walk. Don't take it lying down. Don't throw in the towel. Not now.

You wife may have left you, or is it your husband? One of your children may have been a pain all these years. But see the other side. Your experience can lift someone else from the precipice. You can save a life on the verge. So don't. Remain focused. Stay strong. Don't buckle under pressure. It's only for a season. It won't last long. Others went through the same predicament. Take a moment and read about them. Be encouraged. You are not alone.

You may have suffered bullying years ago. Memories may still linger on. But they are memories to be thrown into the dustbin of history. They serve no purpose now. Remind yourself how you got here. Today is a new day. Tomorrow will even be better. You can regroup, find new acquaintances, and make new friends. You can't be bullied anymore. You can use your energy to help others suffering the same way.

You may have suffered from sexual exploitation and are still haunted by what happened yesteryear. You have remained static. You can't move on, in your subconscious mind. It hurts and is real. But you must decide to move on. To allow healing to take place. To place the burden on another. "Cast your anxiety unto Jesus, for he cares for you." Yes, he cares for you. He has done it for many millions across the world, and he will do it. For you. That is his speciality. That is what he does best. Trust him. Seek help. Trust someone. Share with someone. Now, if you can. You are too precious to let yesterday eat you like gangrene.

Is it your parents you feel you have let down? Years of hate and not willing to forgive? Or you have not related to them as you should? Seems time is running out. Go now. Sort out what needs to be done. They are your parents. Your coming to this world was through them. They cared for you. They loved you. They did more good than harm. Soon they will be gone. And the Bible puts it strong. "Honor your father and mother." This is the first commandment with a promise: "so that it may go well with you and that you may enjoy long life on the earth" (Ephesians 6:2–3 NIV). Respect them, even when you are not respected back. Love them, even though you are not loved back. Provide for them, even though they will never be able to reciprocate it. Go on. Do it. Now! And see what quality time with them will do to your life and to theirs too. There is so much to look forward to. So much in store for both of you. You can build and not break the family. And the world will be a better place.

When Sodom and Gomorrah were razed to the ground, Lot and his family came out running. It was God's doing because of the evil in the city. They went against the law of God and suffered the consequences. Total destruction this time. Abraham pleaded with God. Unsuccessfully. There was no turning back. And the judgement? Fire and brimstone reigned on the city.

This exemplified one of the deadliest and harshest punishments God could mete on a people. Yet out of this devastating situation, God saved Lot and his family. He salvaged a family who was faithful and lived a life that pleased God. This was not the end of Sodom. A remnant remained to carry on.

When Jericho fell, God made sure that Rahab, the harlot, remained as God had promised.

When Elijah the prophet was on the verge of committing suicide, God intervened. Someone may have been unfaithful to you. You have suddenly discovered. You don't trust him or her any more. You are a nervous wreck and don't know what to do. You have sought help, but you hardly trust men, even your pastor. Tough decision to make. You look at the kids, your peers, and maybe church members. Your reputation is on the line. You have a Bathsheba moment. When King David in the Bible committed adultery with Uzziah's wife, imagine what his wife thought. A king sinking so low? A man of God devoid of morals? Irreversible? But God did what he does best. He made David suffer the consequences. The child died. He was condemned through the prophet Nathan, and most importantly, David confessed. God forgave him.

> Have mercy on me, O God,
> according to your steadfast love;
> according to your abundant mercy
> blot out my transgressions.
> Wash me thoroughly from my iniquity,
> and cleanse me from my sin!
> For I know my transgressions,
> and my sin is ever before me.
> Against you, you only, have I sinned
> and done what is evil in your sight,
> so that you may be justified in your words
> and blameless in your judgment.
> Behold, I was brought forth in iniquity,
> and in sin did my mother conceive me.
> Behold, you delight in truth in the inward being,
> and you teach me wisdom in the secret heart.
> (Psalm 51:1–6 ESV)

That was the key for David. He confessed. God forgave him. Deal or no deal? Deal! And that is the challenge for you.

For me. For all of us who find ourselves in the Bathsheba moment. Our response? We emulate God's response. He is our Creator. He has the power to make us cease to be, anytime. But he doesn't, even when we have committed what we can call the worst sin in the world. He loves us so much that after we suffer the consequences of our actions, God comes down and picks us up. Why? So we can tell others and therefore help others who have been in the same position as ourselves to pick themselves up. As David says,

> Cast me not away from your presence,
> and take not your Holy Spirit from me.
> Restore to me the joy of your salvation,
> and uphold me with a willing spirit.
> Then I will teach transgressors your ways,
> and sinners will return to you.
>
> (Psalm 51:10–13 ESV)

The bottom line is that we can, after our restoration by God, turn others back to God. We will be part of God's lieutenants helping him pick up the pieces of other people's broken lives. Hallelujah!

You are a leader who has let your people down. Your integrity is on the line. You feel exposed and naked from the core. The secret has now been let out of the bag. People now know you for who you are: a fraud, a hypocrite. Where do you start? Your children can't look you in the face. A disgraced parent, husband, partner. But God has a plan for you. He has dealt with millions of the likes of you. He never condones but exposes and then reconstitutes the new you. Washed by the blood of Jesus. Jesus did it for you. For me. That disgrace and that humiliation were put on him, so you could be free, unashamed, and proud of who you are in Christ.

So now you realise with Paul of the Bible that "I am what I am by the grace of God." There are some things that only God can do for you. The air that you breathe, the sun that shines, the health that is yours. So you focus on him now. You matter to him and not to other people. You seek to please him. Always. You sort your life with him. Once that is done, you move forward. All else is history. People will still talk, ignore, or just degrade you because of what you have done in the past. But when you have sorted it out with the King of Kings, it's job done and you move on. Acknowledge what you have done and move on. No turning back. God first and then go forward.

In his book *Brilliance in Failure*, Christian A Brickman says, "Do not fear failure, but rather embrace it, take responsibility for it and learn from it. And then refocus to find a new path to success."

When cornered by the rigours and the stresses of life, you find out what really matters. We are too flippant. Mourning over what really doesn't constitute the substance of life. You cry over loss of your job, until you see someone on the verge of dying with cancer. You stress over the traffic jams on a Friday afternoon, until you witness a child tragically killed in an accident. What really matters then comes to the fore when you look at life in its true perspective. We should appreciate more, love more, and be thankful more. Our world forgets the reason for our being: to serve our fellow men and women. To be kind. To enjoy life. Quality life. In our families, among friends and family. Always.

The words of the Preacher, the son of David, king in Jerusalem.
Vanity of vanities, says the Preacher,
vanity of vanities! All is vanity.
What does man gain by all the toil
at which he toils under the sun?
A generation goes, and a generation comes,
but the earth remains forever.
The sun rises, and the sun goes down,
and hastens to the place where it rises.
The wind blows to the south
and goes around to the north;
around and around goes the wind,
and on its circuits the wind returns.
All streams run to the sea,
but the sea is not full;
to the place where the streams flow,
there they flow again.
All things are full of weariness;
a man cannot utter it;
the eye is not satisfied with seeing,
nor the ear filled with hearing.
What has been is what will be,

and what has been done is what will be done,
and there is nothing new under the sun.
Is there a thing of which it is said,
"See, this is new"?
It has been already
in the ages before us.
There is no remembrance of former things,
nor will there be any remembrance
of later things yet to be
among those who come after.

(Ecclesiastes 1:1–11 ESV)

Solomon, in all his wisdom, discovered what life really meant.

Now all has been heard;
here is the conclusion of the matter:
Fear God and keep his commandments,
for this is the duty of all mankind.
For God will bring every deed into judgment,
including every hidden thing,
whether it is good or evil.

(Ecclesiastes 12:13–14 NIV)

When we are broken, we are brought back to the original purpose of our being. A reminder on what we are living for. All else is, as Paul put it, "rubbish." It is when we realise this that we begin to appreciate how valuable we are. We begin to enjoy real life. Our response to what happens to us is transformed. We begin to impact others as we become noticed. We make a difference. We stand out. And our uniqueness shows.

What matters most is good. What matters most will last beyond this life. It is long term. It begins now and ends in eternity. That will not pale into insignificance. Remember what Paul says to the Corinthians:

"And now these three remain: faith, hope and love. But the greatest of these is love" (1 Corinthians 13).

These are the things that matter. They oil the wheel of life. They are permanent and not temporary. You can hold on to these and be guaranteed of a life full of the promises that God intended. The world is in search of these three pillars. They are an endangered species. The world would be a different place if everyone embraced these. All else can pale into insignificance, but not these three.

Don't look back; there is nothing there.

There is always a temptation to look back. Revisit where you have been. Check if everything is OK. In case something follows you. A foe or improper baggage. Things you did yesterday and you are not sure if they are gone. An unpaid debt, an unforgiven friend. There is nothing behind you. It's only a shadow of yesterday. So move on. Set new parameters. Shoot for the stars. In any case, your back is covered by God. He is right behind you. David said God is our refuge and strength, a present help in times of trouble.

Paul in the Bible was clear about the past. He says,

> Not that I have already obtained all this, or have already
> arrived at my goal, but I press on to take hold of that
> for which Christ Jesus took hold of me. Brothers and
> sisters, I do not consider myself yet to have taken hold
> of it. But one thing I do: Forgetting what is behind
> and straining toward what is ahead, I press on toward
> the goal to win the prize for which God has called me
> heavenward in Christ Jesus.
>
> (Philippians 3:12 NIV)

Paul made a deliberate decision to press on. Forget what was
behind so that he could eventually attain his goal. When you
have gone through difficult times and feel a sense of loss, move
on. When your life has taken a battering from the elements
of life, move on. It is a tough decision. It is a scary decision,
but one has to take it like Paul. Remember Paul was beaten,
imprisoned, shipwrecked, and had almost lost hope. But he
used that experience to enable him to help others who were in
the same situation. He says,

> We do not want you to be uninformed, brothers
> and sisters, about the troubles we experienced in the
> province of Asia. We were under great pressure, far
> beyond our ability to endure, so that we despaired of
> life itself. Indeed, we felt we had received the sentence
> of death. But this happened that we might not rely

on ourselves but on God, who raises the dead. He
has delivered us from such a deadly peril, and he will
deliver us again. On him we have set our hope that he
will continue to deliver us.

(2 Corinthians 1:8–10 NIV)

There was no need for Paul to look back. The same God
who had delivered Paul would deliver him again and again. He
is the same God you serve. He is the same God you can trust.
So no need to worry about yesterday, because even if yesterday
does happen again, you have someone ready to help in times
of trouble. You cannot go back again. It won't be the same, for
you are no longer the same.

> You can't go back home to your family, back home
> to your childhood, back home to romantic love, back
> home to a young man's dreams of glory and of fame,
> back home to exile, to escape to Europe and some
> foreign land, back home to lyricism, to singing just
> for singing's sake, back home to aestheticism, to one's
> youthful idea of "the artist" and the all-sufficiency of
> "art" and "beauty" and "love," back home to the ivory
> tower, back home to places in the country, to the cottage
> in Bermude, away from all the strife and conflict of the
> world, back home to the father you have lost and have
> been looking for, back home to someone who can help
> you, save you, ease the burden for you, back home to
> the old forms and systems of things which once seemed

everlasting but which are changing all the time—back home to the escapes of Time and Memory."

(Thomas Wolfe, You Can't Go Home Again)

Lot ran, his daughters close behind. "But Lot's wife, behind him, looked back, and she became a pillar of salt (Genesis 19:26 ESV). She lagged behind. She turned and watched the flaming sulphur fall from the sky, consuming everything she valued. Then it consumed her. The Hebrew for "looked back" means more than to glance over one's shoulder. It means "to regard, to consider, to pay attention to." The Scriptures don't say whether her death was a punishment for valuing her old life so much that she hesitated in obeying or if it was a simple consequence of her reluctance to leave her life quickly. Either she identified too much with the city—and joined it—or she neglected to fully obey God's warning and she died.

Jesus once said to him, "No one who puts his hand to the plough and looks back is fit for the kingdom of God" (Luke 9:62 ESV).

It is sometimes tempting to look back with nostalgia. To the "good old days," to the hurts and pains of yesterday, until the present becomes irrelevant. Jesus in this passage encourages his hearers to focus on the task at hand. To be concerned about what you are doing now and seek to achieve our goals. The kingdom is for the forward looking and not those who mull over yesterday. You should be current and think of today. Plan, strategise, and create opportunities for tomorrow. That is the kingdom strategy. Backward never, forward ever. In warfare terms, looking back in combat exposes you to the enemy. It is a sign of retreat. And you could easily jeopardise the lives of your comrades.

Even when you have reached the end of your hopes and dreams, you still rise up and walk. Your commitment drives you to follow the master and do what he instructs. You don't look back. You can say with Paul, "And I am sure of this, that he who began a good work in you will bring it to completion at the day of Jesus Christ" (Philippians 1:6 ESV). Your hope is built on nothing else but Christ and his righteousness. This is the assurance that you need. Always.

Yet many of us despair. We are double minded. We look back, in case there is something there. We are not sure of where we are going, because we are stuck in the past.

> "This poor man cried, and the LORD heard him, and saved him out of all his troubles."
>
> (Psalm 34:6 KJV)

However broken you are—it doesn't matter how much hurt and pain you are going through—it is when you cry that his attentive ear hears. That cry is therapeutic. It makes a difference.

When you come to your senses, he is still there for you.

God's love is genuine. It is original. Not fake. It is the real thing. It is unconditional. It matters not what you have done, when you did it, to whom you did it, or the circumstances under which you did it. Mind-boggling? And God has demonstrated this through the ages to mankind. We will never comprehend this. But this is the truth.

All God does is wait, until you come to your senses. Until you realise your folly. When you are ready to come back and acknowledge before him what you have done wrong. And you will find him waiting. Arms stretched, ready to welcome you back. That is the story Jesus told of the lost son. After squandering his father's possessions, he came back to his senses and decided to go back to his father. Our story, the story of mankind, is a constant leaving and coming back. However disjointed, fragmented our lives may have become, the message is "Come." However humiliated and exposed you may feel, the message is still "Come." You can never find this philosophy in corridors of power, in the palaces of the most revered king or queen. That is what makes God different. That is what makes the message of the cross unique. That is what makes Jesus's mission statement profound and simple: "to seek and save the lost." His mission was to go for those who had gone astray. Not for the safe and comfortable, the healthy and strong, the confident and courageous.

But God chose the foolish things of the world to shame the wise; God chose the weak things of the world to shame the strong.

And the Bible mentions Jesus as an advocate for those who are deemed sinful. He is always standing, interceding, and pleading in a court of law for those whose rights have been diminished. This is the nature of our God, always at the ready to pick up the broken pieces of men and women who feel neglected and without proper recourse to justice.

This is a unique narrative, a story to be written and rewritten. It is a breath of fresh air to life itself. This is revolutionary. A life changer. Your attitude changes. Your take on life is completely overhauled because now you can see the "me" that you can be despite what you have gone through in life. You can reassess your options now that you have the prospect of living a full life. A life bereft of accusations and counteraccusations from those that seek your downfall. A life full of promises and blessings. This is a life of expectation and hope. A life where the past is forgotten and the future is embraced. A life where you become a source of encouragement to others and add value to those you interact with.

It is when you come to your senses that the dynamism of life kicks in. You can now go back home. Yes, home to your original purpose, your reason for being. Back to where God purposed you to be before the beginning of the world. Back to the comfort of him you can call "my Father" or "Abba." You can go back with nothing but the expectation to receive his love that never changes or fades. His love that never lets you go. It is consistent, patient, ever-present, unconditional love. Wow!

You can now go back to sharing in the suffering and challenges of life from your father's perspective. Back to where you are now identified with your father. His enemies become your enemies. You become the target for persecution, abuse, and denigration.

You become engulfed in the warfare. And that is how it should be, because you are where you belong. The pieces have been put together. You have been made whole and raring to live a life that pleases God. Fully resourced and ready for battle. Are you ready?

Your perspective on life changes when you know that you are fully restored and you have a Father to go to. Your attitude to work and friends changes when you know you are fully restored. Your attitude to your family is enriched when you know you can go back and find love and serenity. You are made whole.

When the lost son in the Bible came to his senses, he said,

> "How many of my father's hired servants have food to spare, and here I am starving to death! I will set out and go back to my father and say to him: Father, I have sinned against heaven and against you. I am no longer worthy to be called your son; make me like one of your hired servants." So, he got up and went to his father.
>
> (Luke 15:17–20 NIV)

We try to help others change by pointing out issues in their lives, but they don't listen. Change occurs when a person gains insight. As long as we are blind to the issues in our lives or we justify the way we are, then we stay the same. But when the light comes on and we see it for ourselves, we are on the road to change. Jesus teaches the principle that insight leads to change in the parable of the prodigal son. Insight leads to change. He came to his senses about his privileges. He came to his senses about his decisions "I have set before you life and death, blessings and curses. Now choose life that you and your descendants may live and that you may love the Lord your God, listen to his voice and hold fast to him" (Deuteronomy 30:15). He came to his senses about his attitude (Matthew 5:3; Luke 14:11; James 4:10) he came to his senses about his sin (1 John 1:9) He came to his senses about his future.

CHAPTER 13

You Can Begin Again

Yes, you can. It doesn't matter how deep you have fallen. It is not significant how way out of line you have been. It may be to do with sin, a curse, or a sheer embarrassment. Your curse. You can start all over again. It's OK. So it does not matter how flawed, scared, or uncouth you are. When God sees you, he appreciates his image in you. The precious you. The golden you.

This song sums up what God can do even when you think you are done and helpless:

> Jesus, my Lord, to Thee I cry;
> Unless Thou save me, I must die:
> Oh, bring Thy free salvation nigh,
> And take me as I am!
>> And take me as I am!
>> And take me as I am!
>> My only plea—Christ died for me!
>> Oh, take me as I am!
> Helpless I am, and full of guilt;

But yet for me Thy blood was spilt,
And Thou canst make me what Thou wilt,
And take me as I am.

(Words by Eliza H. Hamilton;
music by Ira D Sankey)

You cheated, you hurt someone, and you were unforgiving for years. You are a candidate for God's restoration. You are the stuff that God wants. You can begin again. And God takes you back as you are, warts and all. However much you have messed up. Whatever you have done wrong. However much you have not trusted him. He welcomes you. He does not condone what you have done, but he does not drive you away either. He does not treat you as you deserve, for he knows that you are like grass—there in the morning but gone in the evening. In the darkness of your tragedy, in the heat of your chastisement, in the bleakness of your situation, you can rely on God. He will never leave you or forsake you. You may feel broken, but he already sees your reconstituted self. You may feel abandoned, but he sees a restored individual ready to fulfil his destiny. It is important not to give up on ourselves but to realise that God heals the wounds and takes care of us at the point of our needs. No friend, pastor, or relation can do this. They can help by being there, but the activation of the healing process is divine.

When people lose a loved one, it may be difficult to begin again. To live again as before. To appreciate the joys of life now that their loved one is no more. It is hard. But it helps to realise that grieving is OK. Cry as much as you want and do not be afraid to mourn. To hold on to the truth that the Bible gives about death. And there is no need to be afraid to be seen feeling sad and cast down. However, there is need to accept what has happened and to realise that this is what many go through each day. Have moments of quiet meditation and prayer, times of reflection, but don't forget to be there with others. To mix and mingle.

Loss tends to cut deep, and many never recover. They are broken and sadly become the victim of their brokenness. We have all been there. You may be still there, for it is hard to forget the loss of someone you loved. To imagine life without them. A mother, a father, a son, a daughter, a husband, a wife, a boyfriend, or a girlfriend. Time is supposed to be a great doctor. It is meant to heal, but it doesn't. You remain wounded even with the passage of time. Memories linger on. Vivid. Real. Occasionally you dream about the person. You touch them and laugh with them, only to realise it was a dream. Frustrating. It opens up the wound again.

It is a long and winding road back to wholeness. It is a process. But it has to be done. The pieces have to be put together. Life must go on. And sometimes it is important to accept what we cannot change. To acknowledge what has happened and to drum it in ourselves. To know that grieving is all right. And to know that God does not mind if you are cross with him, if you say things you should not say. A friend said to me many years ago, "Tell him what you think, spit it all out, and you can even be mad at God. He understands. One day he will put the puzzle together and you will understand why."

What? Yes, this is the God who picks up the pieces. Jesus cried when he learned of his friend's death. He grieved. So should you. Only be patient with yourself.

It is important to celebrate the life of a loved one who has gone. Recently at a funeral service, the pastor encouraged friends and relatives to treasure the good times and use the memories as a source of happiness. To rally around thoughts of the precious times they had together. They are not gone forever. All we can say to the loved one is "Good night. See you in the morning when the shadows are all gone." This is the Christian hope. They are sleeping, until the resurrection. A comforting thought. No longer broken, but one whole piece again. Wow!

And because God is in the business of picking up the pieces, he helps you go through your difficult times and uses your plan to get you on to the other side.

Yes, you can. It's not where you start; it's where you finish. You are a result of a beginning. A seed in your mom's womb that grew into what you call you. A mustard seed is one of the smallest seeds you can find, but it grows into a big shrub, from its humble beginnings.

Whatever has gone wrong, whatever hurt has been caused, whatever pain has been unleashed on you or on others, you can begin again.

Many people have lost a sense of who they are, through drugs and alcohol. They are shunned by the public and rejected by society. Left in the streets with no hope, but they have begun again. There are amazing stories of many who came to their senses and made decisions to start all over. Deliberate and conscientious decisions to seek restitution and rehabilitation and walk on the rod back to where they belong—humanity incorporated.

Paul in the Bible lived a life of murder, destruction, and persecution. As the history of Christianity unfolded in Jerusalem forty days after Jesus had risen from the dead, Paul and his group were busy persecuting Christians and dragging them in front of the authorities. He caused so much hurt and pain so much that when Stephen, the man of God, was dying from a hail of stones from the crowd, he was there looking after the clothes of those who were taking part in the killing.

But he began again. One day on the Damascus Road, he met his match. He was confronted by Jesus himself and began what was to be the most extraordinary turnaround in history. He was now on a mission to seek and to save the lost following in the footsteps of Jesus, his new master! He became the ambassador for Christ. He started all over again, because Jesus made him to. His decision changed the world forever. You are no different. You can change your world wherever you are.

The lost son decided to begin again when he came to his senses. It was a deliberate, conscientious decision to seek a different course in his life. He weighed the pros and cons and decided on the way forward—home. You may be struggling. Undecided as to what will happen to you in your debilitating circumstances. You may be at the end of the road.

You need to seek life and not death.

I call heaven and earth to witness against you today, that I have set before you life and death, blessing and curse. Therefore choose life, that you and your offspring may live, loving the LORD your God, obeying his voice and holding fast to him, for he is your life and length of days, that you may dwell in the land that the LORD swore to your fathers, to Abraham, to Isaac, and to Jacob, to give them.

(Deuteronomy 30:19–20 NIV)

God gave Moses a choice to choose life or death. This is what is required as you make the decision to begin again. Consider options on the table that in the end come up to two choices: life and death. We should always be aware of this each time we are on the verge, at a tipping point in our lives. It has to be our decision based on information at hand—valid and correct information.

Beginning is the crux of the matter. In the beginning, God created the heavens and the earth. It is back to square one, back to the drawing board. Back to where it started. Regroup and map your way forward from there. The man from the tombs whom Jesus healed was "in his right mind" sitting at the feet of Jesus. And he decided to follow Jesus. Not before he was back to his senses. Not when he was among the tombs. But his mind was back to its normal self. Don't look back; there is nothing there.

Jesus said to him, "No one who puts his hand to the plough and looks back is fit for the kingdom of God."

(Luke 9:62 ESV)

It is not cast in stone. It is dynamic, and it is there to serve God's purpose. So whatever you have been through, and however long it has been with you, you can begin again. Not only you. All of us can. And it is refreshing. It is a new start. Back to square one.

The woman from Samaria, whom we have talked about earlier in the book, thought she was done. She had multiple partners—in fact, five husbands—until she met Jesus. She was offered a brand-new start. Jesus was someone who could quench her thirst. Perhaps her appetite for men. This message resonated with her and—*plonk*—she saw the light. She made a decision to do it again and became an ambassador for Christ. The town was transformed by her message. This was a message of hope, life, and a new start.

What matters is to realise that our God is patient, loving, and merciful. His purpose for creating humans was so that they could worship and praise him, not obliterate them. Like a father, he is not concerned about how much you fail but your capacity to try again and again until you get it. Like a child learning how to ride a bicycle, they will fall from time to time as they get to grips with the skill of riding. In the end, when they get it, the father will be pleased. No matter how much you fail, you can begin again. Back to square one until you accomplish what you have set out to do.

Many have gone through the same route, and the result has been incredible.

> You can begin again. I think that at one time or another, all of us get lost in the middle of our song. A failed marriage, a broken dream, a disappointing career, a financial setback, or a family struggle causes us to hang our heads in shame and wonder where things went wrong. We assume others are watching us like a panel of unforgiving judges, marking our missed notes with enthusiasm. Even worse, we assume God is the head judge, giving disapproving attention to our forgotten melody. With each mistake or setback, we grow ever more nervous, certain we'll receive a failing grade.
>
> (Joyce Meyer, *You Can Begin Again*)

During the armed struggle in Zimbabwe, six missionaries were butchered to death by "freedom fighters." It was tragic. I worked with one of the missionaries who escaped death because he was on a trip to the United Kingdom when this happened. The men and women who did this survived the war. One can imagine the trauma, the stress, and the sheer overwhelming guilt now that the war was over. How could they pick up the broken pieces of their life after all this? Was God interested in them after this? The story of what happened is true testimony to the nature of God and how he does not give up on the people he has fashioned. Writing in a book about the Elim missionary's massacre, the same men who killed the missionaries testified that they had found Jesus.

Eight of them experienced a vision in which they saw the cross and the hand of God coming against them in judgement. Seven of them who had passports immediately left the country and enrolled in Bible schools in West and East Africa. The other one, not having a passport, went to a Bible school in Harare where Peter Griffiths was able to meet him. He had left school at fourteen and had been the youngest platoon commander in ZANLA, operating under the name of War Devil. Peter subsequently kept in regular touch with him. In a separate incident, an African pastor named Mpofu, working for Harare Intercessors, was asked to speak at a rehabilitation centre for ex-combatants in Troutbeck, Nyanga. While he was preaching, a paraplegic man screamed out in agony out of deep conviction, crying for mercy. He later confessed that he had been one of those responsible for killing the missionaries. He told the pastor how the missionaries had prayed for their killers as they were being slaughtered.

They were able to start all over. No guilt and no shame, because Christ had done this for them. There are many stories during many wars in the world similar to what happened in Zimbabwe, but by the grace of God, people were afforded a brand-new start. I can vouch to that. He picked me from the gutter. He showed mercy on me. He gave me my life again. He set me up on a pedestal and launched my new life, with a new vision and new dreams.

God uses circumstances and situations to accomplish his purposes. To restore people. To deal with your enemies and to ensure that his power is realised. When you shudder at what has happened to you. When you are distraught at why you have been put in the environment you are in. This may be a job, a school, an occupation, or a prison. God is there. There is no luck. No coincidence. It is purposeful. It is planned. And it fulfils what Paul says. "All things work together for good for those who are called according to his purpose." The key is to acknowledge where you are. To be determined to understand what it is God wants you to learn through the situation. To know that he can use any situation to accomplish his will. All you need to do is to stay put. To live in expectation. To be positive and optimistic. And to speak hope and not despair. To realise that while broken, God can mend. When you are down, God can pick you up. While in depression, you can experience triumph in Jesus's name.

The thief on the cross had his restoration moment just in time before Jesus went up to heaven. Insight changed his life. He realised who he was crucified with. That he was no ordinary block but the Creator of the universe whose mission was to save the world. It is that insight, that discernment, that can make a difference to our situation. This is the power of recognition. It is important to be on the lookout for such favourable situations, sometimes called "opportunities," when we can grab them and help us realise our destiny.

I was travelling to the USA for a conference and had to pass through our offices in Reading, United Kingdom. During a report session with staff on the situation in my native country, I made a remark concerning the situation. "Even though it is chaotic, but there is an opportunity." Someone picked that up and I ended up being asked to be a member of a university board in the USA, and the title for my first book was derived from that statement. What seemed like a dire situation ended up with great opportunities for the kingdom—impacting others to change their lives or to be restored back to life.

Many people are in dire straits. You may be. Jonah in the Bible was. He refused to do what God had ordered, which was to go to Nineveh. When he did, he was depressed. Jealous because God restored the people of Nineveh after they repented en masse. He was jealous. He wanted to kill himself. But God intervened and Jonah realised the foolishness of his actions. He too repented. He was picked up by a God who cares. A God who understands that we are fickle.

Elijah was at the end of his tether. Downhearted because a woman called Jezebel was after him. He thought he was the only prophet left. Option? To kill himself. Not so fast, God says to him. Many prophets were still alive. Again God picked him up from the depths and he was made whole again. It is when we see ourselves as beyond salvaging that we need to seek God's intervention. To realise that he never leaves us or forsakes us. He is ever present to restore our fortunes.

The world has changed so dramatically in recent years. Wars, earthquakes, and economic crises have many disheartened and despondent. Many millions have no place they can call home. The migration crisis, mainly in Europe, has been dubbed the largest migration of people since the Second World War. Families have been torn apart. Children have been abandoned and others are drowning at sea. Many governments were caught unprepared to respond to such a huge influx of new migrants. Some countries have taken drastic measures like closing their borders and trying to ensure that no illegal people come in. Yet in all this, there is a child abandoned, a mother left to die along the way, vulnerable and disabled people unable to jostle with the others for survival. Broken lives, broken spirits. A far cry from Louis Armstrong's song, "What a Wonderful World" sung ages ago. It is survival of the fittest. A dog-eat-dog scenario. Talk of restoration seems a distant dream. It is the now that matters, including the basic needs of food, shelter, security, and health.

Yet in the midst of such chaos, people have been rescued. Some countries have taken more than their fair share of immigrants. Christian organisations and charities have mobilised resources to ensure that many who are broken are snatched from death's door in the nick of time: the woman on the overcrowded boat giving birth to a lovely girl, the disabled woman in a wheelchair helped to travel miles for shelter, etc. There are many stories of heroism, love, and sheer tenacity. This gives us hope that there is always a way. Never, never, never give up. This may be the difference between life and death.

The Jews felt the same when they saw their temple destroyed. They were discouraged and had lost hope. They wondered if they would ever see the temple in its former glory.

Sometimes when we compare the state of our present lives with our past, we are inclined to condemn ourselves and give up. We say to ourselves that we cannot ever pick ourselves up. We feel defeated and think that it is impossible to restore our lost fortunes and recover all that we had owned. When our life is in a mess, like that of the ruined temple, it is difficult to imagine that we can ever live normal and happy lives again.

God can work miracles in our lives beyond our expectations and imagination. We only need to believe him. In the case of the children of Israel, God sent the prophet Haggai to give them hope.

> Yet now be strong, O Zerubbabel, declares the LORD. Be strong, O Joshua, son of Jehozadak, the high priest. Be strong, all you people of the land, declares the LORD. Work, for I am with you, declares the LORD of hosts.
>
> (Haggai 2:4 ESV)

Sometimes we need to hear other people's stories of hope and not despair. Victory and not defeat. Success and not failure. No man is an island. It is when we draw back into our cocoon that we miss the boat. This is when we wallow in our misery and shame, unable to raise our heads above the sand and cry for help. It is never too late. The time is now. A story is told of a telecast presenter who interviewed people about their problems, but when asked about her life, she broke down. She too needed help but was a facade all her life. When she was asked how she was doing by one of her guests, she broke down. It was the beginning of a realisation that although she sought to help others, she too needed help. And God is using her mightily to tell others the good news concerning God's saving grace. This shows how God can intervene even in the darkest moments of our lives. Sometimes we need to be challenged to help us see who we really are and be able to look in the mirror. As we reflect on who we really are, God reveals himself to us and helps us to walk back to him. To recover and to claim back what we lost over the years. He makes us whole. He shapes us. He restores us.

Sadly, there are many who fail to make it. Their marriages collapse completely. They are never reconciled with their children. And for others, they struggle with forgiving others. They harbour grudges and end up crippled. Some never get healed and live with their conditions all their lives. This is the reality of the situation. Unless something dramatic happens and people change course, the end is not a pleasant one. Yet hope never fades away or ends. Faith still rises above the adversity and burns like a dying wick of an old lamp. There is no time we can say never again or it's finished. For when we do, we lose ourselves and our reason for being. Just like the father in the parable of the prodigal son, we keep looking and hoping. Like my eighty-year-old father talking about my brother who had left home in his teens and had been in Europe for over thirty years. "He will come back one day. I know he will." He did come back, but long after Dad had died. That is hope.

Restoration means back to your original state. The story of salvation in Bible begins with the first couple disobeying

God and being chucked out of Paradise. There was a wedge between God and them and it was impossible to bring back this relationship once again. Throughout history, God devised various means of doing this: through priests, shedding of blood, things put forward as intermediaries to allow this process to begin again, etc. And the Easter story captures the final act by God to restore or bring back the original relationship between man and God. Jesus did die instead of mankind. He suffered on behalf of mankind. He paid the price. He redeemed mankind. It sounds complicated. How would Jesus resolve something that he, in the first place had judged was irreversible?

Your restoration is possible because of God's unending love. As the song goes, "Love lifted me, when nothing else could help, love lifted me." This is agape love that matters even when there is no return to the investment. You still love anyway. Even when enemies do you stuff, you still love anyway. This is contrary to what the world defines as love, which is eros love. God's love makes sure you suffer the consequences of your sin, but still God loves you anyway.

You can never be the same again. In fact, you cannot go home again. Not the same as you were before the salvaging. You are different. You have learned and are ready to impart it to others. God sees the end from the beginning. He knows your potential and is ready to let you lose after the experience so you can help others along the way. Ideally, prisoners, after serving time in prison, are expected to change through rehabilitation. Sadly many don't. It requires a relationship with someone who can mentor them back to life.

Chapter 14

Free at Last

That is the place we all want to be. Free. We strive for it, and many have died for freedom—both spiritual and physical. Total emancipation. William Wilberforce fought for it in the British Parliament. Whatever it is and however long it has taken, when you are free, you are released from bondage: a sick and unhappy marriage, a manipulative situation, a terminal sickness, etc.

When God picks up the pieces of our broken lives, that is his objective. To set us free. Jesus says, "If the Son shall set you free, you shall be free indeed." And he gives life in its abundance. And he does it again and again. He targets everyone. He is not discriminatory. And you are one of them.

There are so many things that bind us, inhibit us, or prevent us from doing what we want to do. Many of us are stuck, gasping for breath. Help seems to be near yet so far. You scream and no one seems to hear you. You have been sounding the alarm for a while, but there is no response. You have sought help from every direction but are still reeling under the hurt and pain. You are bottled in; you are in distress. Like the woman in the Bible who was bound for eighteen years, until

Jesus showed up and cried, "Woman, you are loosed." What a relief. She could let go, at last.

> And behold, there was a woman who had had a disabling spirit for eighteen years. She was bent over and could not fully straighten herself. When Jesus saw her, he called her over and said to her, "Woman, you are freed from your disability." And he laid his hands on her, and immediately she was made straight, and she glorified God.
>
> (Luke 13:11–13)

This is freedom. The opposite of bondage. The ability to do what you were not able to do before. Release as a result of intervention from outside. We are looking forward to this every day. I am. But while this concept is relative in many nations and among so many people, there is ultimate freedom that the Bible talks about. The heaven type of freedom. When the body ceases to be and the spirit takes over and can fly away "to a home where joy shall never end," according to the songwriter Jim Reeves. I becomes boundless freedom. It is the no-holds-barred freedom that Adam and Eve had in the garden. Free to roam about, free to do what they wanted, and free to enjoy fellowship with God. I suppose that is the definition of eternal life. It begins now and ultimately takes us all the way to the heaven that never ends. Joy unspeakable, and the peace that remains and a love that engulfs. Forever and ever. Wow!

You are free in order to bring freedom to others. You are free for a purpose. God's purpose. And the world will be a better place. You may be addicted to drugs or pornography in a way that you feel you are a prisoner. You are broken. What a relief when your help comes. What a relief when you escape from the throes of bondage. It is therapeutic when you can fly away and never look back again. You are vulnerable, and you can't tell. It haunts you. Daily. That is your prison. You feel shackled permanently. Your mind is too. There is no release. The battle is intense. Until someone comes to your rescue. You are like a broken-down car. You are stuck, until help comes on the highway of your journey. That is freedom; that is relief. Not free to do what you want but what God wants. For others. For humanity.

Paul sums up the kind of freedom that is all embracive that God wants. Take a cue from this:

> For though I am free from all, I have made myself a servant to all, that I might win more of them. To the Jews I became as a Jew, in order to win Jews. To those under the law I became as one under the law (though not being myself under the law) that I might win those under the law. To those outside the law I became as one outside the law (not being outside the law of God but under the law of Christ) that I might win those outside the law. To the weak I became weak, that I might win the weak. I have become all things to all people, that by all means I might save some.
>
> (1 Corinthians 9:19–22 ESV)

This is mature freedom. It's not arrogant but humble. Not exclusive but inclusive. Considerate and not abrasive. Sensitive yet open and transparent. When God has picked up the broken pieces of our lives, we become truly free. We are not ourselves but we serve others for the glory of God.

The graphic picture of the man who lived among tombs who met Jesus illustrates clearly what is meant by freedom. He was chained. He was living in tombs. Not of his accord. He was traumatised. And each passing day was a drag for this man. Until he met Jesus. He realised the possibilities when he encountered him. Suddenly, he could envisage his shackles being removed. And they were. He sat at the feet of Jesus "in his right mind," fully clothed. Demons scrambled for cover. Normality had come to him. At last he could do things he never did before. He was now able to socialise and for once recognised Jesus for who he was: the King of Kings and the Lord of Lords. He was now free. So can you be. Now. Today.

Are you free? Be thankful. Tell others about the process. Has God picked up your broken pieces? Now is the opportunity to demonstrate to others what God can do. You were saved in order to save others. Burdens are lifted at Calvary. Remember the thief on the cross with Jesus? His guilt and his shame were done away with in an instant. He got an invitation to join Jesus in heaven that night. Wow! Surely there is nothing impossible with God. Any situation is redeemable. Any conflict can be settled. Any guilt is erasable. Any shame can be rectified.

The blind man in John 9 testified to this. He was born blind, but when he met Jesus, he saw. His testimony is an expression of how transformed he had been as a result of what happened to him. Unfortunately, the religious leaders, instead of celebrating his deliverance, accused Jesus of healing the man on the Sabbath. Not everyone will celebrate your freedom. Many will want to remind you of yesterday, but you will not take notice of them. Enjoy your present and live life to the full.

And this is what happens when you experience freedom. Not everyone sees it or appreciates it the way you do. Instead of celebrating, people rationalise. Instead of acknowledging the miraculous, people point fingers. A tragedy of a world in which we live. It can happen. You can be free. It matters not how it happens and where it happens. The important thing is the transformation, the solution to the problem, the release from what was to what is. That is what matters.

Freedom is when we acknowledge that without God, we are nothing. That our sins or our inability to measure up to God's standards meant that we were ostracised from our maker. Realise that it had to take God's initiative to enable us to go back to our original status. To curry favour with him. It was an act of sheer love and mercy that made God become man that restored our relationship with God. And simply put, God's love became so overwhelming. He became the Lamb of God that takes away the sin of the world.

So the process of freedom involves acknowledging that we can do nothing without Christ, admitting our shortcomings and asking Christ to forgive us. Then he releases the power to free us. We are given abundant life, which is for us to enjoy for the rest of our lives. We can then truly shout, "Free at last!" Many have gone through this route. Many are healed restored and forgive. They have a future full of hope. They can walk without fainting. They have discovered themselves. In the process, they have helped others do the same. This is real freedom, real forgiveness. It is not fake but genuine.

When God has dealt with you seriously, it means you have gone through the refiner's furnace. Once the experience of who has touched you happens, and you hear the words "Thou art loosed," God's dynamic intrusion unfolds. Your pieces come together. You don't feel but know the deed has been done. Not by man but God himself. No wonder why David wrote many songs of praise to the God who had freed him from danger, endured battles with him, and helped him escape the fowler's snare.

If it had not been the LORD who was on our side—let Israel now say—

if it had not been the LORD who was on our side when people rose up against us,

then they would have swallowed us up alive, when their anger was kindled against us;

then the flood would have swept us away, the torrent would have gone over us;

then over us would have gone the raging waters.

Blessed be the LORD, who has not given us as prey to their teeth!

We have escaped like a bird from the snare of the fowlers; the snare is broken, and we have escaped!

Our help is in the name of the Lord, who made heaven and earth.

(Psalm 124 ESV)

You can sing this song with David, you can experience his deliverance, and when you are free, you know it. Like a bird, you know you have escaped. You know who let you out of your life's cage. And you are grateful like David. And it is forever. This is my experience. And I am forever grateful to God. I can walk tall. I have confidence that I am what I am by the grace of God. Even though I walk in the valley of the shadow of death, I shall fear no evil, for God is with me.

You need this confidence. You need this courage. The all-present realisation of what you can do through Christ. Of your status and position. Knowing that because you have been rescued by the Creator of the world, nothing will separate you from the love of God. That you can do all things through Christ who strengthens you. Come on, don't be lethargic. Don't be afraid. Go for it. Do whatever God has told you to do. Serve others. Inspire others. Motivate the fainthearted. Be a beacon in a world that finds no solace. Be the newsmaker as people observe God through your life. Stand out and demonstrate your uniqueness.

Others have sought fake freedom. They have pretended to be free yet hurt inside and preached freedom yet still are in the fowler's snare. You ought to be different. And the panacea? Knowing God and all that he has promised. Sticking to the tenets of God. Reflecting on who he is and what he has done for you. Living the experience of forgiveness and forgiving others too. Loving others as he loved you before the foundation of the world. Being a reconciler just as Jesus reconciled us to God. And treating others just as you want to be treated yourself and adhering to the greatest commandment of all.

You are called upon to love the Lord your God with all your heart and with all your strength and with your entire mind. And love your neighbour as yourself! That is vertical and horizontal love, always. That is the character of those who have been set free. Accountable to God and to fellow human beings. You can't go wrong. You are on the right track. And a world full of such species is transformational, progressive, and life-changing. This is as it was meant to be. And this is true freedom. Strive for it, protect it, and go for it. Now. Today.

Sadly, many people have decided to run away from the freedom that God offers. Instead, they serve their own selfish interests outside what God has made available, for reasons that include ignorance and a desire to do their own thing. The rich, young ruler suffered the same predicament when he failed the test of true freedom.

> The young man said to him, "All these things I have kept; what am I still lacking?" Jesus said to him, "If you wish to be complete, go and sell your possessions and give to the poor, and you will have treasure in heaven; and come, follow Me." But when the young man heard this statement, he went away grieving; for he was one who owned much property.
>
> (Matthew 19:20–22 ESV)

What prevents you from experiencing true freedom, now that you know that your pieces can be put in place again? What prevents you from implementing your plan of action, when the resources are at your disposal? Do you need to seek the help of others to steer you back to your chosen path? Remember God is qualified to do so. He has restored many in the past, and you are no exception. Jesus came that we might have life and have it in abundance. Wow! It may hurt so bad, you may still struggle with forgiving someone, your illness may still linger on, but stay focused. Focused on the One who can make a difference, now and always. You are a winner, a conqueror. That is what God promises us all.

When you are set free from your struggles that have dogged you for years, you are forgiven, you should scream freedom. Jesus said, "If the Son shall set you free, you shall be free indeed." And the history of men and women over the ages experiencing such freedom is awesome. Drug addicts who became dry after a battle with addiction, some suffering from terminal illnesses who went into remission and were declared healed. And some who, though they still live with their condition, have found freedom and release from the stresses and strains of the disease. They have come to accept that which they did not wish on themselves. Now they have become ambassadors for the cause. Marriages that had collapsed under pressure but were revived when two people decided to bury the hatchet and move on. Children who had left home and vowed never to come back, but in typical Prodigal Son fashion, they came to their senses and came back home.

Yours has been a journey as well. You have your highs and lows. But the greatest assurance comes from the fact that you can rely on a God who has proved himself. A God who is competent enough to deal with our troubles and tribulations. A God who cares for us so much that he is always on the lookout to draw men and women to himself. To pick them up and restore them to their former glory. Your response? Walking and leaping and thanking God.

And it's OK for you to shout loudly and clearly, "Free at last; free at last, thank God I am free at last."

The End

Remember life is a journey, from the cradle to the grave and beyond. It begins with God and ends with God. You may be broken along the way. You may contemplate quitting midway. It's OK. You are not alone. You will meet fellow strugglers along the way. They have been hurt and abandoned and some are on tenterhooks through depression, stress, and loss. But remember you are special. You are unique. He who created the universe is in the business of picking up the pieces. Your pieces. So take advantage. Hold on to him. Stay focused, and you will be made whole again. You can begin again. You can be restored, so go for it. Let God pick up your pieces. Now!

Printed in the United States
By Bookmasters